T0158757

Working with the Emotions

Jigme Rinpoche

Other Works by this Author

A Path of Wisdom, Rabsel Éditions, 2012
The Handbook of Ordinary Heroes, Rabsel Publications, 2016

Working with the Emotions

Jigme Rinpoche

RABSEL
PUBLICATIONS

Working with the Emotions
Compiled from 3 series of seminars at Dhagpo Kagyu Ling,
May 1994, 2002, and 2003

RABSEL PUBLICATIONS
16, rue de Babylone
76430 La Remuée, France
www.rabsel.com
contact@rabsel.com

This project was supported by the DRAC and Normandy Region under the FADEL Normandie, France.

ISBN 978-2-36017-011-1

Table of Contents

Introduction

Implicit in any explanation on 'how to deal with the emotions' is the acknowledgement of the undeniable impact that the emotions exact in our lives. The Dharma shows us the methods to 'take back' control from our emotions, and be free of their hold on us. We could only achieve this freedom by applying the methods and undergoing a process of change. It is a gradual inner change in our mind that will witness a decrease in distractions, and disturbances. This reduction allows our mind an opening where understanding of the causes of the emotions, how they influence us in our thoughts, speech, and action, becomes possible. Moreover, this understanding shows how our whole perspective of this world and ourselves are colored by our emotions. As a result, we will come to fully appreciate the importance of knowing our own true nature. We will understand why the Buddha stated that all living beings are in a state of ignorance trapped in the conditions of samsara. We will be able to discern clearly our inner conditions, our inner veils that obscure our view at the present time. Then we can choose. Through the clarity of mind we can discern what is important, and beneficial for ourselves and others. The concepts and perceptions that distract our mind and cause us suffering now will become transparent. We will know them precisely so they could no longer sway us. We will recognize the need to change our habits and tendencies and how to change. This means we will know how to balance our mind. We are then free. Above all, we will realize how all beings equally are caught up in the same way by the emotions. This view in-itself is indispensable to a genuine appreciation of, and a commitment to Bodhicitta, or enlightened mind, a mind bent solely on benefiting others. And it is Bodhicitta mind that will lead us to reach perfect wisdom that is awakened mind.

1 - Towards Awareness

The human mind has the capacity to reflect on the meaning of life and who we are. We are capable of understanding the nature of life described in the Dharma as 'samsara'. The Dharma books explain in great lengths the conditions of samsara, such as suffering, impermanence, and karma (the law of cause and effect). Each of us individually has to examine the relevancy and validity of the Dharma in our own lives, only then would its true meaning come to bear. To understand the Dharma is to understand the fundamental conditions of a human being. When we try to see more clearly, certain meanings will become apparent to us. For example, we will see how we live our lives unconsciously following the rules of society, and our inner tendencies. Mired in everything around us, we are not aware of what goes on inside us. By paying more attention to our inner functioning, we will begin to get a real sense of what life is all about.

Of course, in the beginning, it is not easy to reflect, or to be aware of our inner workings. We are simply not used to it. It is always when we are in a bind that we pay attention and try to figure a way out. Unfortunately, after the problem passes, we go back to our old ways. And we haven't changed. The teachings tell us to go deeper when we are faced with difficulties. Use the experiences to understand better the way we are. Use our conditions, and our experiences as opportunities to learn how we function. If we could do this, then without any pressure or force, quite naturally, we will begin to feel a sense of who we are. Moreover, it is possible that we will discover a different way to be.

Avoid the trap of temporary methods

Our problems seem endless. As soon as one problem is solved, another is at our doorsteps. Individually, we use various methods to cope with the many situations. These measures relieve us somewhat of our immediate dilemmas. They could make us feel better temporarily. However, our makeshift solutions are not effective in eliminating the difficulties.

To cope, some people suppress, or ignore their problems, which just keep resurfacing. On the one hand, the temporary solutions we devise are necessary. They help us deal with the various issues confronting us. On the other, we should not rely solely on them. If we do, then we are wasting time. It is better to get to the roots of the problems, and clear them out. For example, you have a back pain. The pain is a symptom of your back problem. You go for acupuncture to relieve the pain. A few days later, the pain is back.

A medical doctor once explained to me that it is important to treat a diseased body organ, and not only the symptoms of the disease. The necessary remedies should be taken until the organ is healthy again. The same applies to mental pain. Suppose you had just argued with a friend. You feel disturbed and annoyed. Feeling unhappy, you go and listen to some teachings, or talk to a Lama, or a therapist. When you feel better, you think, "*I'm OK*." And you leave it at that. A few days later, you find yourself again in another argument. The point is you don't forget it once you're feeling better. The Dharma is a very effective remedy, but you have to continue to take it. Then one day, your problems will truly be over.

The very great Lamas all faced difficulties when they first set out on the Dharma path. They persisted in their practice and applied the meaning of the Dharma consistently all the while aware of their samsaric predicament. Then very slowly they reached the point where they were able to solve all their relative problems. Still, they continued to progress in their practice and eventually attained some realization of wisdom. Then without hindrance, they continued until they reached the ultimate goal. This shows how they had found a treatment plan for their ailment, stuck with it until they were completely cured.

No question, the process is long. Gampopa and other great teachers all confirmed this. So we can relax. We don't need to rush or to worry either. Taking our time to walk step by step the Dharma path, we apply the teachings and continue to do so day by day, in a relaxed way.

Ignorance gives rise to illusion

A fundamental truth underlies all Dharma teachings:

every living being has a basic potential called Buddha nature. You may consider your habits, and your capabilities as your potential. But actually, there is more. There is Buddha nature. We could think of it as our basic potential. We are not aware of it due to a fundamental obscuration of mind called ignorance.

Ignorance does not mean stupid. It refers to our inability to see and to understand clearly. We are unable to realize our basic nature. In this way, it is as if our vision is impaired. Unable to seeing properly, we follow our own ideas, and our feelings. As a result, we don't know what is really important. In fact, by running after our inner urgings, we are further developing our blindness. We are building up our ignorance, and getting further away from seeing clearly. Unknowingly, we are creating more harm, more negativity, leading to ever more suffering.

The Buddha discovered that everything is our illusion. Our perception itself is the illusion. At the moment, we may think we know a lot about things - the ordinary everyday things. But really, our knowledge is unclear and fragmented. Yet, we experience our ideas and thinking as truths. In fact, we are ill-equipped to understand the full extent of reality at the moment. We have no choice but to live our tainted perceptions or illusions ensnared by myriad of emotions and the suffering associated with them. We cannot do so much. Even to listen and reflect at a deeper level, or to grasp the precise meaning of the Dharma proves challenging. Otherwise, if our perception were perfect clarity, then simply reading the Dharma books would enlighten us. For now, we may think we understand while the exact meaning eludes us.

To step back, listen, and reflect

There is a way that sounds very simple, simple to hear but not so easy to apply. It is to practise being aware. Try to step apart from yourself and watch your thoughts, and actions. Try to listen and be aware of your feelings, reactions, and ideas in you daily encounters. Discuss among friends the various conditions, or difficulties that you do observe in yourself. Listen to each other more carefully as you recount and share your experiences. Ask questions of one another, and really listen to the answers. This means to get the meaning rather than just hearing the words. Use the Dharma as your reference. You need to practise a lot of inner reflection and introspection. It will take time, and the result will not be immediate. Nonetheless, it is really beneficial to reflect whenever possible, and to continue to do so every day.

When you refer to the Dharma teachings, you will find many beautiful songs and poems. You will find many philosophical terms and concepts, which seem all very profound to you. Not barring the fact that they contain very important meanings, do not be trapped by the poetic language and imageries. Rather, ask what is the exact meaning being conveyed? What do the words say about the causes of our actions as human beings? What do they say about the inevitable results/outcome with respect to karma? You are not used to reflecting like this. But try to understand more precisely, this is the point. It will bring you good results. By understanding the different conditions of yourself (or others) in terms of cause and effect, you will come to understand all the conditions of samsara. You will be able to see very clearly. You will see or understand how to deal with the distractions and disturbances in your life.

In the beginning, to listen and to reflect on the meaning of the outer or inner conditions is difficult for you. You are not used to it. You are used to following your established ways every day. You have never given pause to try to really reflect. And you have never really examined the Dharma practically in the ordinary everyday incidences. You may feel you have understood the meaning when it is really your own feeling of it. The Dharma sounds so simple and right away you feel you have got the point. But you have not got the exact meaning. This is the main problem. Your current habit of mind has intercepted your understanding. Therefore, try to look deeper when possible. Without undue pressure, pause, think, and question more deeply. Slowly, you will become more familiar with the various thoughts, concepts, dialogues, and feelings in you and around you. Then you will start to get the meaning. Step by step, and very gradually, this more in-depth reflection will be acquired as a new habit. The more familiar you are to looking deeper into the meaning of things, the clearer you become. The meaning will appear to you quite effortlessly. It is in this respect that this approach is considered simple.

2 - The Emotive Causes

When you hear the word, 'emotion', you associate it with certain feelings you experience. It may be a feeling of fear, anger, grief, happiness, or excitement. The feeling can be physical, mental, or both. In the Dharma, it is explained that any emotion first appears as an agitation, or disturbance in the mind. This initial onset has the potential to further develop, so it is 'the cause' of something to come. Because the disturbance could develop into an emotion or feeling, it is more precisely, 'a cause of an emotion', or 'an emotive cause'. In fact, we have a Tibetan word that means just that.

There are three primary emotive causes all connected to our ego grasping. They are ignorance, desire, and hatred. Different combinations of these three in varying degrees give us pride, jealousy, expectations, and many other emotive causes.

Now let us look at what happens to an emotive

cause. To help us understand, we use an electric circuit as an analogy. The electricity is analogous to the disturbance, or emotive cause. If we understand about electricity and we know how to work with it, then we could wire the circuit properly to a light bulb. We would have light, which is useful to us. But if we don't know how to connect the wiring and we get ourselves caught in the middle of it, then we have put ourselves in harms way – we could get electrocuted.

The point is to first understand and then to know how to handle an emotive cause. This would enable us to respond in a constructive way. For example, we could use an emotive cause like pride positively by recognizing that we are again grasping to ourselves. Using Dharma as our reference, we know that pride will bring us suffering if we follow it. We choose not to, and instead, we try to be more considerate to others. On the other hand, if we are not even aware of our pride, if we don't understand what pride could do to us, or we don't know how to cope, then it could develop into an overt arrogance, or worse, pride could justify outright acts of violence. Therefore, how we deal with an emotive cause actually determines the outcome, be it positive, negative, or neutral. It is very important that we understand this point.

The teachings tell us that the emotive cause comes first, then afterwards the feelings, or emotions. The terms, 'feelings' and 'emotions' are interchangeable. For instance, when you say you are happy, you mean you feel the emotion of happiness. When you are unhappy, you feel the emotion of suffering. But feelings of happiness, unhappiness, and other emotions are all developed from emotive causes. They are the 'responses' to the emotive causes.

Unfortunately, in most translations from the Tibetan, the cause of the emotions, or emotive cause is translated as the 'disturbing emotions', or 'negative emotions'. The cause aspect is actually lost in the translation. Moreover, the adjective, 'negative' presupposes 'negative results only'. The emotive cause is not immediately negative per se. True, it is a disturbance in mind rooted in our ego clinging and our fundamental ignorance. In this respect, an emotive cause is considered negative because that it can lead us into negative actions, ending inevitably in suffering.

Naturally, your understanding comes from the words you read or hear. In turn, your understanding determines the success of your getting the proper meaning in any given situation. Suppose you follow the descriptive, 'negative emotion'. When you next detect 'desire' arising in you, immediately, you will judge it 'negative'. You will try to get rid of it. You will try to suppress it. Both are wrong approaches. What is worse is you lose the opportunity to understand your desire. But if you understand properly that your desire is an emotive cause, then you know you still have choices as to what to do. Discovering the emotive cause (by yourself) in your own awareness, you will not be caught/trapped by it. Using the Dharma as your reference, try to keep this understanding in mind, and your awareness will follow correctly.

The emotive causes are a part of our human condition. They are not bad per se. As a matter of fact, if we look closely enough, the roots of our emotions can be positive. We are the ones who unknowingly turn them into something negative. For example, after work, you are driving home on the highway. There is a traffic jam and you are stuck in it for over half an hour. All of a sudden, the guy in the car next to you drives onto the shoulder and speeds away. You know he will be home in no time, and you're angry. Why? "*He should not have done that. The shoulder should be used only for emergencies. He's going to cause an accident. What if we all did like him? Imagine the chaos and dangers!*" At first, you are reasonably mindful of highway safety. But very rapidly, the emotive cause of aversion deteriorates into a form of jealousy. "*Why should he get away with it? I could do it, too, and why not me? I am late, too. I should not have to lose out.*" By now, your internalization has escalated into a stronger emotion of anger. Then when you get home, while you are explaining why you are half an hour late, you call the man a 'name' while recounting how he took off on the side. Your valid awareness of his irresponsible driving has degenerated into an outright hatred towards him. This is how we allow an emotive cause to grow into something quite negative.

Emotions cause us problems

The emotions are often the subject of many discussions and teachings, because they disturb our mind and cause us much unhappiness. They taint our perception thereby altering, and distorting facts. Going by our feelings, we make wrong choices, hurting people around us. They cause us much frustrations and worrying. We would all agree that at times, they render us feeling helpless and exhausted. Under their influence, we do harmful things to one another. For example, I feel disturbed by someone, and I am not happy. In turn, I say something mean and hurtful to someone else. On the other hand, pleasant circumstances make me happy, and so I can be very nice to others. However, neither the 'meanness' nor the 'niceness' lasts.

Happiness and sadness are feelings we experience.

Of course, when we get what we want, we are happy. Nevertheless, if we really give it more thought, we will realize that whatever our gain, we will face its loss. It will change or break down. The same applies to our feelings. One moment, we feel happy, in another, we are sad. Yet the point is not to feel nothing either. The point is not to suppress our likes and dislikes, but to recognize that we do live our lives in this way. Our happiness is momentary, so is our sadness. It is very important to see clearly how we are. Otherwise, a lot of confusion could set in and we have no idea what things really mean, good or bad. Our distractions and disturbances of mind, and our problems, too, will never end.

Aware of ego clinging

To practise the Dharma means to be aware of ego clinging, which is at the root of all the emotive causes. The clinging triggers the emotive causes. They in turn produce tensions, which fuel or develop our feelings of stronger emotions. We feel disturbed and unable to have mental calm. We are unhappy. The Dharma shows us the way out. It starts us out with this basic recognition, "*I can develop by myself the awareness of all the emotive causes which are controlling me at the moment. I can choose to be more aware in the present moment so as not to fall under their control and influence.*" This is in fact the crux of Dharma practice. It does not mean that meditation is not useful. Most people think Dharma practice is meditation. That is true, too. Meditation is very important. It helps us to develop our awareness. But if after two hours of meditation, you go out and disturb everyone around you, then your meditation is not serving a purpose.

There is a trap that we have to avoid and it is self-centredness. We always consider ourselves and ourselves only. "*I am doing something. Here I am looking inside myself.*" In fact, we are the problem. If we are not aware, we run the risk of further developing ego grasping. To be free of this self-concern, we connect with Bodhicitta. We have to consider others are at least as important as ourselves. In any and every action we undertake, we do it for the well-being of others. "*If I look to understand myself, it is only to enable me to understand what takes place in others as well. Then I could support them and help them in an appropriate way.*" The emotions and their causes function in the same way in everybody. Consider also the fact that our actions affect others just as their actions affect us. In this way we are all interconnected. This recognition alone will help to reduce the intensity of our emotions and ego grasping.

Being able to care for others does not mean that we don't have ego grasping anymore. Some degree of it is always present but our point of view is shifting. And that is the point. Beyond our own self-interest, we will begin to care to support other people. We don't throw our garbage out the window because there are other people around us, for example. Together, we try to keep the roads clean. People who litter are concerned about their own convenience. They don't really care that other people share the space, too. If they cared, they would not litter. This shows how our attitudes determine our actions. When we are aware, we would naturally not do certain things out of our concern for others. The effect is we are developing Bodhicitta. As well, the presence of Bodhicitta makes our emotive causes more apparent as well as those of others. In time, this recognition of the emotive causes make us feel more relaxed, such that we could see more clearly what is needed in any situation.

To want to change

To begin with, we have to want change. We don't want to be controlled by our emotions anymore. We have to want to find ways to deal with the emotive causes. Take 'studying' for example: if you have a real interest in learning, you will enjoy studying. You will study day after day and will develop a taste for it. Very naturally, you will continue to study to expand your knowledge. But a student studying just to pass an exam, would much rather be at the beach or a club. To him, studying is a drag. He does not feel the reason or the need to study. Therefore, he will not, on his own, take to studying. The same applies to working with the emotions. We have to really want to be free from the suffering of emotions. Otherwise, we would not want to do something about it.

Through our own personal experiences, we first become familiar with how we function. When we are aware, we have a chance to adjust by ourselves. The Dharma tells us that this is indeed possible. We can change. We can learn how not to be disturbed by our emotions and feelings. We need the proper means. We follow the proper methods. Suffering will decrease due to less harm being done. Suffering is the result of harmful actions. We are reminded to always refer to the teachings for guidance. We have to reflect carefully on what is 'harmful'. What are the causes of harmful actions? Very gradually, our understanding will increase, and our mind more open. Our actions will be more positive, our communication and interactions with others more useful and beneficial for all. This brings us to the very importance of developing Bodhicitta mind because it is one of two conditions (the other is meditation) that enables us to effectively deal with the emotive causes.

3 - Bodhicitta

Bodhicitta, often referred to as 'enlightened mind' or 'enlightened attitude', is generally translated in English as 'love and compassion'. Bodhicitta is a natural quality in us not apart from our mind. It is mind solely oriented towards benefiting others. It is much more than 'being altruistic'. Actions that are seemingly alike on the outside may be differently motivated. The results of these actions will accordingly be different. We cannot judge based on appearance alone whether someone is acting out of Bodhicitta or not. Perfect Bodhicitta is enlightenment expressed in action. It is neither a cover, a concept, nor is it separate from the action itself. Uncontrived and completely unfabricated, Bodhicitta in action carries none of the usual frustrations encountered in ordinary action.

We are careful in our understanding that Bodhicitta is not meant to be displayed in a 'show-offish' way. It is not a public demonstration of how someone is now dedicating his life to others nor is it a form of martyrdom. As explained before, because Bodhicitta is naturally in our nature, there is really nothing for us to show-off. There is nothing to create but a gradual development of a quality that we have already - an open willingness to care for others. Some people may find it difficult to even imagine this complete openness of mind. We begin by learning to perceive things in a different way. If we know how to look, then things will start to appear differently to us quite naturally. Therefore, it is really important that we should first see the meaning of Bodhicitta for ourselves even if we do not yet know how to apply it. Next, we should know exactly why we need to develop it. Then, we should learn how to develop it. If we are properly directed in these three ways, we will find it easy to change. Otherwise, our current confusion will be endless.

Beyond our own perspective

When you question why Bodhicitta is necessary and important, you may come up with an answer suited to your liking, or to your own interpretation of it. This is normal. You are always following your own 'take' on things. In fact, the Dharma is very easy to agree with because it makes sense. It seems easy to follow. Therefore, when you actually try to develop Bodhicitta, your personal perspective will most likely be reinforced. Knowing that your own interpretation of the Dharma might get in the way, you should try to be aware of your own biases.

On the whole, you will find that you agree with the Dharma. However, an inner rejection, or resistance to the teachings might still linger inside. Take your time to reflect deeper. To gradually open to yourself takes time. Why do you even have to be cautioned or reminded of this? It is because you have a tendency or habit to resist first that which is unfamiliar to you. We are all like this. We tend to follow our habitual tendencies thereby missing the important points. We may have a flash 'got it' experience, but the next moment it is gone. We are right back in our familiar ways. Of course, we think we have understood already. So we need to reflect more carefully to ensure that our understanding is as clear and as precise as possible.

Some aspects of the Dharma might instill some fear and discomfort in us. Our inner resistance makes it difficult for us to listen properly. Why? Because we are so used to escaping from our problems, and to avoid any unpleasantness. Unfortunately, it is very necessary to wade through the difficulties. To face and deal with our troubles is in-itself a step in the positive direction; we look to the Dharma for the many methods and tools to help us deal.

See the conditions of beings for Bodhicitta to arise

We may question why we have to feel love and compassion towards all beings. The answer lies in truly understanding the conditions of beings as universal with no exceptions. This means to see the conditions we all experience. One example is how our emotions play a role in the way we think, speak, and act. Bodhicitta will arise in us very naturally when we really recognize we are under the influence of our emotions. The absence of this recognition blocks our connection to Bodhicitta even if we wanted it. What the Buddha saw is quite different from our view right now. When the Buddha taught about the conditions and problems of beings, he was not referring only to the incidences of difficulties we face from time to time, rather, he saw the conditions that were global, and applicable to every being in life. One such condition is the inability to see clearly. People often try so hard to be honest. We all try to do our best, yet our efforts often create more difficulties, and suffering because we cannot see clearly. We don't know what to do. The Buddhas, and the Bodhisattvas see the true conditions that we are in. They see us engulfed in our difficulties, unable to get free. Very naturally, they feel deeply compassion and love for us and so they tirelessly expound the Dharma for our benefit.

Unfortunately, nobody could show us how to see. We have to do it ourselves. Therefore, using the Dharma as our reference, we take the time to analyze and to examine the conditions of ourselves and others around us. For example, on the surface, everybody seems very nice, very sincere, very kind, and wishing to be helpful. But somehow, due to not-knowing, more often than not, individuals cause more harm than good. Some people create many ideas, they carry out many activities and projects in the name of 'helping'. But their self-serving motives create harmful consequences immediately and ensuring more suffering to come. For example, someone who is familiar with the justice system may find ways to manipulate it to his own interests. He uses the law to hurt people who are unaware of the intricate legal details. He gets them in trouble with the law to achieve his own agenda. His negativity is serious dragging others along with him creating long term negative effects for all. In this way, he is the 'bigger' criminal. Yet he is totally unaware that he is the one creating much suffering. He thinks he is on side with the law. And so just as the Buddha said, beings living in samsara unknowingly perpetuate the cycle of suffering.

To develop Bodhicitta, we need to see more clearly into the conditions of living beings. In order to start seeing more clearly, it is helpful to be aware of some veils, which may block and distort our view. We could refer to them as screens in our perception.

The screen of judging

We can feel love. We can feel compassion. But our love and compassion differ from the Bodhicitta that the Buddhas and Bodhisattvas have for us. The difference lies in the presence or absence of discrimination, or judging. Discrimination is absent in the enlightened beings whereas 'judging' occupies our mind far too often. Our kind of love and compassion arise out of discrimination. When we love, it is emotional. It is linked with desire therefore not entirely sincere. This kind of love brings you suffering. You feel that you can love yet actually it feels more like a 'mask' that you put on. So you have to try to see clearly, then you will come to realize how you are actually creating your own suffering. What does this mean? It means that true Bodhicitta, how you love, and how you feel compassion, depends very much on your inner orientation. Bodhicitta directly connects to your views and attitudes. You must therefore be very clear about them.

If you find the meaning of Bodhicitta quite difficult to grasp, you are normal. Your constant judging limits your view and narrows it down to discrimination, to duality. *"This is right. This is good and I like it like that,"* or *"It should be like this, or like that."* When you are wrapped up in thinking dualistically, you cannot conceive love and compassion. Although the ability to discriminate does reflect some clarity of mind, nevertheless, the constant judging is more distracting than clarifying. Instead of always seeing differences, try to see that all beings are basically equal, in that we are subject to the same conditions. Then, we will be more balanced, and our perception clearer. We would then see what is needed, what is important, and what to do.

The effect of seeing clearly is greater freedom, freedom from the suffering and freedom from the non-clarity. Judging blocks you from seeing clearly. Reality thus eludes you. You are at odds with reality, so you reject it. This means you are once again caught in your trap. It is a continuous cycle. You are again unhappy and you suffer much confusion. This is why to see clearly is very difficult. You have to curb your tendency to jump to conclusions, or to fall back on what you are used to. Instead, question and probe deeper to get the point. Again, and again, you have to keep trying to go deeper into the meaning. Without proper understanding, any progress will again be interrupted. This is why you are always stuck repeatedly, because you have not really got the meaning. For example, the Buddha taught the Four Noble Truths. When you first heard about them, you might not have thought that life was 'so much' suffering. You might have felt that there was some suffering. Then you started to look more carefully. You paid more attention to the experiences you encountered and those of other people as well. Then slowly, you would realize that what the Buddha said was completely true. Then you are really experiencing and seeing the conditions of suffering. You are fully convinced. And you will look for solutions, and a way out. This is what is meant to discover the meaning by yourself, step by step.

The screen of shortness of view

Another difficulty is that our vision is too short. We cannot see far into the future. This is why we cannot fathom or appreciate the real meaning of karma. We are also not very patient, and we are never satisfied. These 'not so desirable traits' are perhaps our habits or they might just feel natural to us. But they pull us back from true understanding. We don't feel like trying to see differently. When we can't understand, we give up right away. As far as suffering is concerned, we try to avoid as best we can. We try to run away if we can. Temporarily, ignoring or suppressing our problems might appear to give us momentary relief. Regrettably, this is precisely why to this day, the problems are still with us. As much as we don't want to suffer, we do not really care to understand it in order to be free of it. Why do we not care then? It is because we cannot see the consequences of our actions. Our vision is too 'short'. So our effort is correspondingly 'short'! Where our effort is required, we always feel it takes too long. But if we could extend our view farther, we would understand that what seems so long now is actually a brief instant in the time continuum. It is all relative. We question why we have to put in so much effort. Unable to see farther ahead, we resign ourselves to feeling, 'whatever for?' Yet at the same time, we cannot bear any suffering.

On the other hand, for some brief happiness, we are all too willing to put in as much effort as we can. Regardless of how long it'd take, we'd do it, during which time we'd endure all kinds of mental stress and pressures. We are willing because we want the momentary happiness. Of course, due to our tremendous effort, we do often succeed in achieving the appearance of the happiness we sought. However, it is but short-lived. It does not last. For example, a Tibetan dish of dumpling takes three hours to make but all ten minutes to eat and more fat to gain afterwards. It is the same with any work or any project that people do. During the making of the dumplings, there is some anticipation, some desire, but the process is not an emotionally negative one. But in business and in other forms of work, people work very hard under much stress, suffering, and the influence of the disturbing emotions. The end result is always short-lived. Once one goal is reached, it is on to the next one! And the short-term results also continue to appear, and then disappear. Try to see if this applies to you, too.

Be aware of your own strivings. Try to be aware of your attitudes, effort, and feelings as you work for what you want. Also, look at the results. At first, you might feel some inner contradictions. You might feel somewhat disheartened to recognize that the end results or rewards are short and transitory compared to what you have to do and give up to get them. When you try to be aware and look, you will run into the same problem again of your 'not seeing' too clearly. Therefore, you have to refer to the Dharma and try to make sense and logic of it. If you check, and reflect in this way, step by step, you will come to see how you were influenced by various conditions in your past actions and experiences. It is very important to learn from your past - to see how you were conditioned to do as you did, and still do. This insight will make you understand the meaning of the many things in your life. You will see how you view things, and how you are attached to things. How you want things, and how your wanting bring up the emotions. The opposite of wanting is rejecting. Your aversions also make you emotional because they are one

28

form of attachment. You will really come to a genuine understanding of the meaning of samsara. Even if your aim is not enlightenment, you will still understand how the emotions distort your view. You will see the meaning and the causes of your emotions. Therefore it is really worth your while to look.

See your own conditions first

In order to see the conditions that we are in, we always begin with ourselves. To understand about love and compassion we also start with ourselves. And the process will take some time. Look at yourself. Your pride and ego clinging obscure your mind. However, you should still try by using the Dharma as your guide. Try to reflect on how you are. Reflect on how you think, how you deal with situations, and what you consider important or not. What do you want for your future? Here, future refers to this life as well as future lives. Looking at yourself, you will be able to see in greater details about the emotions, the suffering, and the causes and effects of things. Very gradually, you will see more clearly the conditions that influence you and trap you. You will then realize that you must do something to free yourself from their hold. As you understand more, you will apply more effort, which will lead to deeper understanding. The clearer you are, the more effort you will apply in the right direction - to be even clearer.

As a result, your clear understanding about yourself will allow you to understand others as well. Why...because they are also subject to the same conditions as you. Ever so gradually, you will begin to see the meaning of 'illusion' of which the Buddha spoke. He described how we are caught by our illusions. Following our illusions, we have many hopes and expectations. We act to fulfil them while creating more karma. And so life goes on for us as we act and live through the results of our actions. Not everything is negative. People, in general, try to be good. Inadvertently, they cause more harm than good because they are unaware of the causes of the emotions. So they are led into negative actions. This is why not to be disturbed or influenced negatively is fundamental - neither by your own emotions nor by other people's. You will feel differently once the emotive causes become increasingly transparent to you. Your mind will be more at ease so you will be able to deal with everything.

Understand karma

To develop Bodhicitta, we have to know and see clearly the conditions of all living beings. Where do the conditions come from? The conditions themselves are the results of karma. We have 'karma' means we live the conditions brought about by our past actions. Everything has a cause—the infallible law of karma. Things do not come randomly out of nowhere. They have an origin. And the result is linked to this origin. When we have experienced by our own perception the validity of karma, then we would always take it under consideration in whatever we do. When we listen to the teachings, we sometimes feel an inner resistance to understand and to adopt Bodhicitta. We don't want to do it. We don't want to face it. In a way, we want to forget about ourselves totally because the teachings seem quite heavy. To follow the Dharma is really hard work. But step back a little, and ask yourself what Bodhicitta really means?

Bodhicitta, does not mean anything other than to see things truly as they are. Again, what does that mean? It means that everything has a cause. A result comes from a prior action. We try to be mindful of the fact of karma. We have all touched or experienced something that is bright yellow/orange that produces heat. It is fire. We always recognize fire and its attributes. We know it can burn so we keep our distance. It is the same with karma. We have to really know it for ourselves. We have to touch it and experience it in our own lives—time and time again until we are convinced of its validity. For example, once we notice that we are in fact happier when we are less engrossed with ourselves, we will learn to relax. When we know that frustration comes from caring too much about the self, we will learn to release our grip. Besides, we never really get what we want when we are selfish. We cannot be happy. Caring for others makes us happy. When we really see this direct correlation of karma clearly in our own experiences, we will naturally help and support others. Even when we are busy helping others, we feel satisfied. It gives us a very good and important reason for living. Moreover, through our commitment to others' welfare, we will uncover our own basic potential, or wisdom, or Buddha nature. The Buddha said, more than 2,500 years ago, that looking for one's own happiness leads to suffering and making others happy leads to enlightened mind. In others words, to go 'all out' to benefit others will lead to our own liberation.

It is fairly easy to be convinced that we are actually happier when caring for others rather than for ourselves. For example, just one week before your vacation, you are thinking so much ahead to your holiday that the week becomes unbearably long. As a result, you could not wait for it to be over. Another scenario for that same week sees you focused on doing something for somebody else. The week will likely pass quickly.

Even when we know we cannot be like Mother Teresa, who was a great Bodhisattva, we could still help in our own ways. We could smile more for instance; try to be friendly with one another without fighting or arguing. We could adopt a proper attitude, a kindness towards others by noting their qualities instead of focusing on their shortcomings. We could stop thinking of ourselves exclusively and start caring more for others. In this way, our own frustrations will decrease effectively improving our view of things. Unfortunately, our society leans towards self-centredness in exact opposite to openness and benevolence. This is why Bodhicitta mind has to be explained. We have to consciously make effort to connect with it because it is Bodhicitta that would produce everything that is good.

Karma is not all negative. There is positive karma, too. It is the negative actions that cause suffering. We can easily see the very many sufferings around the world, some people experience tremendous suffering. Relatively speaking, ours is not as bad, but nonetheless, we experience significant suffering in our individual lives. If we could truly appreciate the fact that suffering is a universal condition then we would be able to grasp the meaning of Bodhicitta. This point cannot be emphasized enough. There are two different aspects with respect to our human potential. On the one hand, it is our natural capacity as humans to feel love and compassion. On the other hand, our very self-focused, always ego-clinging mind creates much pain and suffering. As a result, we find it hard to embrace others through love and compassion. This is why we have to reflect, practise, and meditate in order to gradually develop a real understanding of Bodhicitta. It is not so easy because it involves a true opening of oneself to others, and not just some fleeting moments of rational understanding. True understanding of Bodhicitta is crucial because it installs in us an ability to deal effectively with all the emotive causes.

4 - Working with The Emotions By Applying Bodhicitta

The emotions constitute one of the main subjects of the Dharma teachings. In the Vajrayana, we often hear the expression: 'to transform the emotions into wisdom'. Unfortunately, the translation is not very precise. We really should not expect that we could transform our emotions into wisdom. This wrong expectation will block our understanding of the real meaning of the terms. Rather, we keep in mind that our aim is to go beyond suffering. And to attain this goal, we try to connect with our wisdom, our basic potential.

At the moment, due to our mind's ignorance, we rely heavily on our limited perception, which is compromised by all kinds of conditions. If we were to leave everything as is based on our impure perception, the suffering would be endless. Some may argue that there are joyful, happy moments, and positive things going on, too. But these are still rooted in attachment thus inca-

pable of delivering any lasting satisfaction. Due to impermanence, we always feel that our joys are short-lived
while difficulties feel more like our mainstay. But beyond the positive or the negative attachment is wisdom.
If we connect with wisdom, and apply it, then eventually, we would attain a state beyond suffering, and beyond
ignorance. But even before we reach the final state of
complete liberation, there are enormous benefits to be
had. For one, we won't be so affected by our emotions.
Our emotions are usually centred around issues with
people. It is through our relationships with others that
we get ourselves entangled. At times, we feel that if we
could only stay quietly somewhere by ourselves, then
maybe the causes of emotions won't arise anymore. But
isolation is near impossible these days, and the problem just goes dormant anyway. Sooner or later, it will
surface again. We are connected to people and things
everywhere, so we can't really avoid them. Our involve-
ments with others are therefore endless so we have to
learn how to cope. The practitioners who have reached
certain levels of realization attest to the fact that Dharma practice is effective in loosening the grip the emotive
causes have on us. It facilitates a deeper understanding.
It renders clarity of mind. It shows us a different way
to use our emotional states, the proper way. We would
then know how to cope positively given any condition.
Our suffering is thus reduced. The results always come
step by step, very gradually, over time.

To deal with the emotive causes and the emotions
without Bodhicitta as our base would be an artificial
and temporary remedy much like taking a painkiller to
get rid of pain. The pain would come back. It would not
end. Likewise, without Bodhicitta, our aggression or anger closely linked to ego clinging, the source of many suf-

fering, will also not end. Many people who are religious might appear kinder than those who are not, but underneath the surface, hatred still looms. The negative conditions are still continuing. One wrong word, a seemingly innocent remark, and a kind person changes into a very angry one. The conditions for suffering were never gone. Therefore a profound understanding of Bodhicitta, and of all our conditions is indispensable. The good news is change is possible. It is possible to understand the meaning of our emotions, and their causes.

See the cause of our feelings

We do not suppress our emotions nor do we get rid of them. The emotions and their causes are a natural functioning of our mind. In the same way that we don't stop a train by standing in front of it, we don't stop the emotions by force. We don't cover them up with our hands and tell them, *"Don't come out!"* We have to see them more precisely. This means not to conceptualize about the emotions but to try to understand how they arise, how they are sustained, and how they agitate the mind. This kind of recognition entails more than a mere intellectual understanding because an emotion is neither produced by the intellect, nor is it a product of external conditions. An emotion is entirely from within us, an inner feeling. It is a symptom of our ego clinging. Each of us feels distinctly that 'I' exists, separate from others. 'I' will feel emotional depending on the circumstances as they relate to the 'I'. Therefore the 'I' is at the root of the emotion. I am happy, for example, means 'my self' is happy. So in fact, we have a chance to recognize the ego grasping through the manifestation of the emotions. It is really worth our while then to seize the chance when an emotion such as anger arises to delve deeper into it.

What does this understanding do for us? It gives us the ability to know naturally by ourselves what to do. It is just like when we feel cold, we put on a sweater; when we feel warm, we take it off.

When we feel happy or sad, we don't see the underlying causes of these feelings. We feel happy but we don't see the desire, which caused us to feel happy. We feel angry but we don't see the hatred that makes us feel like that. The next time when you feel upset, angry, or afraid, try to see the link. What is the underlying cause to your feeling? In the beginning, this is quite difficult. You are not used to it. Take the example of your feeling upset because somebody said something not to your liking. You might try to be patient and not say anything. This is good. But afterwards, try to see where your dislike came from. What caused your disapproval? Its emotive cause could be pride. It could also be due to your expectation, or desire. This shows how the emotive cause may be different each time you feel the emotion of dislike and vice versa.

The emotional response to an emotive cause also varies each time depending on the situation. For example, the emotive cause of hatred could develop into an actual emotional feeling of 'hating', 'resenting' or 'feeling uncomfortably agitated'. Another example: pride as an emotive cause could develop into the emotion of anger. Pride could also develop into a feeling of happily prideful or arrogant – walking around with our nose up in the air. You could explore your whole range of emotions – what are their underlying causes, how they develop, and how they subside.

Through your own observations, and experiences, you will come to understand that your feelings are linked to the different 'emotive causes'. You will begin to see the correlation between your emotive causes and the shaping of your perspective. This in-itself means your seeing is becoming clearer. You are not free yet, but you will begin to get the meaning of 'illusion'. In time, you will understand why the teachings say your mind is obscured, and that you follow your illusion. It is like believing in something unreal and then following the false belief. If you were drunk, or high on drugs, you would realize afterwards that what you had experienced was not real. 'You were under the influence.' You would dismiss it as a 'distortion' - in other words, an illusion. Similarly, while we are under the influence of the emotions, we feel what we experience is real. Our ego grasping is strong so we have to gradually learn to see the causes of our feelings, i.e. the emotive causes.

It is difficult to be constantly on the lookout, which actually adds unnecessary pressure. Try to look from time to time when you are in a situation that is not too disturbing. What are the conditions and circumstances for your agitation? Do not pick a time when your emotions are already proliferating for the obvious reason that you won't be able to see. In the beginning, your strong habits and usual tendencies may block you from seeing how your mind is. But little by little, you will start to see more clearly. Then you will get a different sense of how you actually function.

To develop our awareness

In fact, recognizing an emotive cause could occur quite naturally. The problem is often we are not really conscious of what takes place. We lack awareness. Even the times that we are aware, we are still unable to detect the very subtle emotive causes flowing underneath. In order to heighten our awareness, three things are to be developed.

- First, do not daydream about anything other than what is in the moment. For example, when we are listening to a teaching, we should not be thinking about the fallen trees during a storm, or the pizza we are going to have for lunch. We should be concentrated on what the teacher is saying. This is the first point to be developed.

- Second, maintain a constant and correct motivation for being aware. We should appreciate the importance of awareness. We see awareness as a 'must have'. Without it, nothing is possible.

- Third, develop a relaxed mind - neither sleepy nor drowsy. We wish to develop a mind very relaxed but clear.

Any time is a good time to be aware of how an emotion functions but some occasions are more suitable. It is when things are going relatively smoothly that we tend to forget about the small bumps. We think they are normal and so nothing is wrong. Instead, we pick a time when things are falling apart to look. Unfortunately, it is also a time when our emotions overwhelm us. To be able to observe them calmly is near impossible. We bring our car in for regular checkups and minor repairs. We don't wait until our car is broken down to fix it. It is the same with our emotions. Don't wait until we are falling apart in a crisis to try to see what is wrong. The training of how to deal with emotions should happen when we are mildly angry, or slightly jealous - we try to comprehend how the external causes could create such annoyances, and disturbances within us. The energy of the emotive causes in fact comes from us even though the causes appear to be 'out there'. It is 'I' who is reacting to the externals. Through the very little everyday agitations, we will begin to see this truth. Of course, we could also introspect when everything is going right, but generally, it is the bumps that make us sit up and take notice.

Frustration is linked to our motivation

Most of the time, we are actually strengthening our emotions. When we are not happy, we tend to look outside for the reasons. "*I am jealous because he got promoted instead of me.*" We feel a certain way because of someone or some event. We are like this all the time. But we could change. If we look at the emotions themselves, they are not so important. And the external factors that we assign to our emotions are also not that important. In fact, every time we are confronted by an unpleasant situation, we can react differently instead of our norm. In other words, we can choose to be relaxed and think for others.

The idea of Bodhicitta, or just being able to open more to others is foreign to some people. They cannot act with this open mind perhaps because they do not see any reason for it. What is the benefit in acting with loving kindness? More interestingly, ask what is the disadvantage in not acting with Bodhicitta? The fact is acting out of self-interest alone inevitably leads to unhappiness and suffering. We should see if this assertion is true in us and in others. The self-importance or self-focus fuels the emotive causes thereby producing stronger emotions and in greater numbers, too. As a result, we find ourselves at full speed going from one emotion to the next, expending much energy and revving up the tensions that consume us. Satisfaction is impossible and we suffer. As soon as we get something, we are on to the next thing, and so the rush continues.

It is different when we act out of concern for others. The action does not require as much energy because the emotive causes connected to the 'self' are in check. Our desires and aversions even when aroused are not too intense. As a result, we don't feel too sad when things don't go 'our' way. We don't feel so excited when they do either. We could afford the time to think clearly giving proper consideration to the situation and doing things properly. Tension is kept at a minimum. Where there is no expectation, and where we have the interest of others at heart, there is no cause to feel unhappy. We feel satisfied in doing what we can. One of the excellent results of working for others is our ability to open to others quite naturally. The net effect is we are more comfortable with ourselves and in our relationships with others.

There are often different reasons for doing something. Ask yourself, "*Why do you do it?*" "*Because it has to be done,*" may be your answer. But your motivation could be varied. You may do it for your own benefit alone, or for the benefit of people in general, or for people you know. Accordingly, in each case, depending on your motivation, your expectation will be different. And an unsuccessful outcome would affect you quite differently.

If you act simply because you have to, then if others are hurt in the process, it is just too bad. You are not too careful because you feel you have no choice to begin with. The result is all that you're after. When something goes wrong, you will feel very frustrated feeling it's a waste of your effort. The same applies when you act solely for your own benefit. You'd feel even more frustrated when you fail because of your personal involvement. You may/may not be conscious that your action will hurt others. By the time you realize that harm has been done, you excuse yourself claiming that it was not done on purpose. But, the effect of your negative action could not be erased in both situations. The parties involved including you, will suffer negative consequences as a result.

When you act considerate of others, and things don't work out, you are naturally much more willing to let it go. You know you wanted to help, and so you did. You have already achieved at least that part. Your frustration is not as strong as in the previous two scenarios. Since you have taken others into consideration, your action will most likely not harm them. The possibility of a mistake is therefore much less.

Even a chore like washing the floor, or cleaning the house, if you do it because you have to, then, you'd much rather be doing something else, something more fun, better, easier, and less boring. However, if you do it so that your family can enjoy a clean house or for your visiting friend, then it becomes your offering to these people. You will do it with heart and enthusiasm. Same action, but different motivation: the ego-centred way, or the openhearted way. The choice is yours.

In general, when things go our way, we feel fine. If not, we feel sad and miserable. When we are arguing with someone, it is always the other person's fault. "*He is not doing what I want.*" In short, we want our way only. We don't have to take ourselves so seriously. When things then go a little wrong, we can deal. Again, good or bad depends on our motivation. It is important to note that our action may still turn out to be the same—with or without our concern for others. The absence of self-interest enables us to better cope with obstacles. We are not trapped into fixed and narrow points of view. Things no longer have to follow exactly and perfectly in the way we want them to. This relaxing could only come about when our self-importance is considerably diminished.

Most of the time when we encounter a snag in a situation, how we experience it actually depends on us alone. This does not mean that things will work out if only we are kind and we 'keep smiling'. Some people try to keep the mind peaceful by blocking out the problems. Both these views are wrong. We do not use Bodhicitta to gloss over the difficulties. This is not at all the point when it comes to applying Bodhicitta. The point is by being considerate of others, we are naturally more relaxed and the immediate benefit is that we could be more effective in managing our affairs. Take for example, a volunteer translator at a teaching. The volunteer recognizes that his work is useful to people who cannot understand Tibetan. He is happy to do it for others. He is relaxed and tries his best, and he feels satisfied. But if he considers himself a good professional translator, then he will care about the quality of his translation. He is therefore not relaxed checking himself and thinking of ways to improve. Before long, he finds himself discouraged, and would rather be outside doing something else.

Bodhicitta lifts us from self-confusion

The amazing thing about the Bodhicitta mind is that

the emotive causes can neither disturb, nor change it. It is quite unlike our mind engaged in ego-clinging upon which the emotive causes wreak havoc. This is why it is so difficult for us to see clearly when we are blocked by our own confusion. The only way to free ourselves of ego clinging is to turn our attention towards others. Then we will have a chance to recognize how our emotions influence us.

The next time you get upset because you think someone wrong, ask yourself, "*If I apply Bodhicitta now, what difference would it make in how I feel? And how would I feel if I choose to ignore Bodhicitta?*" If you are not terribly angry, you can see your reaction in both scenarios. You will realize how effective Bodhicitta is in deterring ego clinging. It prevents you from being exclusively self-focused. It lifts you from duality – from pitting the 'I' against the 'other' fueling problems and aggression and suffering an inescapable result. By engendering Bodhicitta, somehow all the oppositions no longer appear as menacing to you.

You cannot think like the Bodhisattvas right away. You cannot turn into a saint overnight. You apply Bodhicitta accordingly at your own level now. You can only feel love and compassion at a level that comes naturally to you. It should not be forced. But if you could only muster as much as a single percentage of Bodhicitta, it will give enormous benefit. It will solve a lot of problems of the mind. The benefit of whatever your actions, or contacts with others, would be manifold.

In the Bodhicitta prayer, we pray that we'd do as much as we could. This means in keeping with our individual capacity, and understanding. It is not that we must do exactly as the Bodhisattvas or we'd be failures dropped off of the Path. We follow the Bodhisattva Path step by step at whatever our level is now. In this respect, it is simple.

The two questions to ask

Everyone lives life differently subject to individual conditions. Basically, all we want is to live peacefully and happily with our family. We wish to get along well with our friends and with the people at work. We all hope to be productive and useful in our lives creating something important for everyone. We never set out to irritate people, or to create problems for ourselves. We desire harmony and happiness. However, we always have problems, not big problems but the little irritants and distractions of everyday life. Ask yourself why there are always these disturbances. Most people accept them as normal. The fact is we are really not too clear about them. We don't really know. The Dharma tells us that these are the conditions of samsara due to ego clinging. When you try to look at your own conditions, you will find that some are solvable but most of them seem impossible to solve. If you use the Dharma as your reference, if you reflect, and probe a little deeper, you will find that you don't need to fight, argue, criticize, use strong words, have outbursts of strong emotions as often as you do. They are not 'must-do's. It is very important to find out why they are not necessary. Using the Dharma as your guide, question your attitudes, your way of thinking.

"Do your attitudes contribute to your self-grasping?"

"Do your attitudes allow you to support others?"

These are two very simple questions. With every condition, or every situation you encounter, ask yourself these two questions, and you will know what to do every time.

For example, when you argue with someone, even someone you like, you are very emotional. You are actually suffering yet you accept the feeling as natural in any argument. Your inner rational is you really just want to help whatever the situation is. But reflect more carefully and you will see more clearly. Are you just grasping to your own views and desires? If you look, you will see that there are two different approaches. Your wanting to support the other and do what you can is one. The other is that, very often, hidden underneath is your unconscious wish to use the other, or your reluctance to lose your position. You might also expect the other to agree with you. These attitudes are very strong and hard to detect at first glance because you are quick and adept at concealing them in your own defense. Again, taking the time to reflect very carefully, step by step, you will come to see them. *"Yes, I do have attitudes that are self-centred. I do have these feelings of wanting my way. Quite honestly, the problem is with me due to my grasping to my desires, and wanting attention for myself. This is why I reject others and react the way I do."* In general, we can see more or less how we function but we are not really convinced yet. This is why it is so hard for us to change. If you really see your inner attitudes, you will see them arising and then dissolving. It is very strange - you know your thoughts, yet you cannot work with them. What this means is you have not understood clearly their meaning. You may understand them in a rational way but not yet at the feeling level. It takes time. It is not easy. But it is actually possible.

Remember impermanence

The teachings tell us that our grasping is very deep. It is there, ever so subtly. Ask yourself why your mind grasps and attaches to small and big things alike. Its direct effect is your perceiving things as solid and permanent. You feel you still have a long time in life when in fact time is neither long nor short. It is ever passing, changing. It does not stay for even a moment. But we don't see it as such because we are under the illusion of permanence. We feel everything is permanent. This is why our desires and attachments are strong. To change this perception is very difficult. It also happens to be our major problem. By understanding the impermanence of everything, our whole focus will begin to change. If we don't understand properly, we might feel frightened. But if we make a real effort to be mindful of impermanence, this will give us another view, a real insight into how things are, and not just an artificial understanding.

The conditions of beings are alike

Something happens, right away, you mind is grasping. For now, your mind tends to grasp at everything, a condition of 'always wanting'. This accounts for the constant distractions, a magnet for more negative causes. You are also suffering. But you don't see the suffering. You are too convinced, too sure that 'this is right'. Try to analyze the meaning of 'right'. Refer to what the Dharma says, and you will come to realize that being 'right' is your feeling. Try to project what will happen if you simply follow your feeling of right. You can refer to your past mistakes when you had followed what you thought was right. The more you see, the more meaningful your understanding. The benefit is your ability to let go of many things that used to bother you. Right now, you cope by suppressing, or looking the other way whenever you are in a conflict situation. It works to a small degree but the problem keeps coming back. If you can see clearly, then you will be able to let go.

By watching yourself, you will soon come to realize that everybody really functions in the same way. You may perceive that somebody is acting negatively. If you really analyse the root cause of his actions, you will discover it is due to his ignorance. He doesn't know. You may think yourself quite nice, and proper. But at the same time, deep down, you know you are fully capable of committing the same negativities. It's just that you can see the reasons for not doing so. Actually, this means that you do understand why he did what he did. This insight alone forestalls hatred for the person and prevents you from feeling hurt or angry. Moreover, the insight is indispensable to you if you were to feel love and compassion for all beings alike. You must understand the basic causes of their suffering. If you find it difficult to have compassion, then it means you are not seeing how you function. The two are interconnected.

When you can understand the mistakes of others, you start to understand ignorance and the illusion wherein you are caught. You will see that though on the surface, every being is unique in character and patterns of behaviour, underneath it all, the basic causes and conditions of all living beings are subject to karma. The individual is 'lost' because of the fundamental ignorance or 'not seeing'. Through this, you will start to feel compassion. Things become much clearer. As a result, you are actually more peaceful. Of course, the problems and difficulties are still all there, but you are not so disturbed. You feel more encouraged to help. When you can't see, you are reluctant to help people who are acting badly. You take the negativity personally. Take the time and effort to understand others more deeply. Then very gradually, you will see increasingly their conditions. The effect in you is a real appreciation more than ever, the goal of liberation.

Not as an escape from suffering

Even though Bodhicitta is key to our being able to deal with our emotions, it does not mean that we use it to escape from our emotions or to stop them. Some people think that in order to reduce their own suffering, they should try to make themselves feel Bodhicitta. *"To reduce my own suffering of the emotions, I am going to develop Bodhicitta."* This does not work. Why? Because the feeling of Bodhicitta comes from an actual seeing and understanding of the universal conditions to which every being is subject. We will then act in response with this proper understanding. This is how it works. All the different ways of practice boil down to this very essential point.

We don't get it

You know there is ignorance. You know there is suffering. You know about impermanence. You understand the importance of Bodhicitta. When all these elements have been integrated into your view, the emotive disturbances will become much more pliable and easier to work with. You will see how you live connected to the emotive causes and your feelings, which will not disappear. They are with us constantly distracting us due to our habits of mind. The good news is they are also changing in the moment.

You may acknowledge that being free from suffering is very important yet you cannot do it. The main reason is you don't see the conditions you are in. You don't understand them exactly. And the teachings explain that until we have grasped the meaning of all our conditions including the emotive causes, it is difficult to be free of them. This understanding does not come immediately. It comes about step by step unnoticeably at first. Only until considerable time has elapsed do we have a sense that the way we feel has changed.

It is very easy to say that we want to be liberated from samsara. But in fact, by talking like this, we are dwelling ever more on it. Our wish to become liberated becomes an attachment, a temporary desire. If we look carefully enough, we will see that while we'd like to be liberated yet at the same time, we'd rather not. This is what it means, 'to be caught up'. We are not yet convinced that going beyond suffering is the most important thing. True, we feel leaving samsara is important but not just yet. Individually, somehow, each of us is still very much focused on samsara. This shows that we have not yet got the point. And because everything is linked, our '*not getting the point*' permeates all aspects of how we are in the world. If we really see that for every action, there is an inevitable result, then we will know for sure that the results will be endless because our actions are endless. Even if we could not comprehend what enlightenment really is, we will feel the urgency to steer in a different direction. Step by step, we will realize that not to be influenced by the emotive causes is tantamount to being free from samsara.

5 - A Spiritual Path

In Buddhism, to be 'spiritual' means to strive to be clear, conscious, and capable of understanding everything. You are not distracted, or disturbed. Your mind is peaceful, and you are able to act and work with any situations, conditions, or circumstances in a harmonious and constructive way. 'Spiritual' does not mean magical, powerful, or affecting miracles. In Buddhism, we talk about peace and harmony. We wish to be beneficial and useful. These conditions come about through our ability to work with our own minds. In the absence of proper understanding, difficulties and distractions are the order of the day.

Everyday you are engaged in many things. You may find a little time on occasion to practise. If this describes you, then your main focus is likely not the Dharma. . You agree with the different Dharma theories. You know. You understand...but somehow you still don't know what to do, how to apply the teachings in your life. The Dharma is neither theory nor intellectualization. The meaning of the Dharma comes through to each one of us at an individual and personal level. To get the meaning, we need clarity. To have clarity, we need to practise regularly.

Often, we try to do too many things. There are many Dharma methods. One method alone gives good results. All that is required is a little time and effort on a consistent basis. Even when we know a particular method works somehow it is not enough; we have to go searching for more. The fact is we are losing time. If we could stick with one practice, we'd be able to solve all the problems. You may not agree but many successful practitioners would attest to its validity. It is an important point to keep in mind, and to see if it applies to you.

Life as a spiritual path

When we work with the causes of emotions, we always use the Dharma as our reference. Our tendency is to nestle in a comfortable state of mind. Unconsciously, our attitude is to use the Dharma to cope with difficulties. We follow the advice to learn about our inner conditions when we are really more interested to solve our problems. We think that when we are emotional, we would then try our hand at 'transforming' the emotion, an idea we have picked up from the teachings. In our mind, this is 'applying the teachings' when in fact, we have just picked up another wrong concept. A proper approach to the Dharma is to connect to it as a spiritual path. To live in the Dharma means that we live every day to develop harmony with others. We try to be always helpful and useful to them. At the same time, we try to maintain a peaceful state of mind within. Then very gradually, we will achieve a capacity to liberate ourselves from ignorance and from the suffering of samsara. This is what the Buddha taught. This is the essential practice of Buddhism.

The Buddhist path as a spiritual path consists of, not just one, but numerous methods to achieve the same goal. In the Buddhist centres, many methods are taught. Some methods are relatively easy while others might prove quite challenging. Everyone can choose a method. But to know how to choose, it takes time, patience, and effort to understand the meaning of the Dharma properly. And then it takes time, patience, and effort to follow a right practice. But it is possible to find a right practice and then to develop it, which is really what it takes to follow a spiritual path.

The Dharma path is not easy for Westerners, Asians, and Tibetans alike. Even when we try to engage devotion, and perform positive actions, purification and merit accumulation, we still encounter many difficulties. Why? Because as human beings we are deeply connected to samsara. And what the Buddha taught feels contrary to our samsaric ways. We are used to gathering knowledge and achieving results. This is how we live. But Dharma practice requires a different approach and therein lies the difficulty.

We may practise out of curiosity at first. We are unable to really fathom the importance of the Dharma. We feel it makes a lot of sense. But when it comes down to really working with the methods, it is not easy. Our mind cannot get the meaning right away. We have to meditate. As we meditate more, we will appreciate increasingly how important the Dharma really is to every single one of us. Our understanding occurs in layers.

Layer by layer, we will delve deeper into the Dharma's meaning. Our understanding will expand, and our clarity will increase. We will encourage ourselves to meditate and to continue. And the more we do, the clearer the meaning; the more important the Dharma is to us, the more motivated we will become, and the more we will do. This is how it works.

Dharma practice is not a duty

We must not regard Dharma practice as a duty. We should not pressure ourselves excessively. The teachings explain about the 'good' and the 'not so good' actions. The explanations are for you. They apply to you, to your life now. The Dharma is not just theories and principles. You are told that certain actions will bring certain results. Really examine what that means in your own life. Based on what you are doing now, what kind of results will you achieve? Practising the Dharma does not mean to follow and obey rules and regulations. Often, you stop questioning when you feel you have understood the general meaning. But try to continue to question why the Dharma says what it says. *"If I follow the teachings, what benefit will it bring me? What benefit will it bring to others? If I act negatively, what are the consequences relative to me and then to others?"* Little by little, try to get clearer. Don't just stop when you are a little clearer. Continue. Examine and evaluate the meaning either through self-introspection or through discussions with others. This process also enables you to begin to notice the emotive causes and influences in you. Unaware, your long established tendencies and habits would continue to sway and block you.

References guide us on the Path

When you begin to practise, you may find it very difficult to focus and concentrate continuously. But actually your whole life can become your Dharma practice and not just the times you consider as practice. This applies to everyone and it is very important and good to apply the meaning of practice in every aspect of our lives. But we need direction. If we have no reference points, then it'd be difficult to find the way. To do extensive research on our own is very time consuming. Therefore we rely on the Dharma so we won't get lost. The teachings themselves are very simple to follow. But we have to beware of the complications we tend to create for ourselves. Be on the lookout for the screens of judging, shortness of view, which have been explained earlier, and the distortions created by our emotive causes.

It is sometimes hard to observe ourselves but we could learn a lot by looking at the people around us to see why they behave and act as they do. We apply the Dharma because it gives us many pointers. When you look, you'd find that some people could not really act properly. Some people act properly, but they could not do the practice properly. Then there are those who don't even think about the Dharma. Your observations are neither critiques nor fault-finding, rather, they serve you like a mirror to see and understand about yourself. You could observe the Sangha, your friends, and people in general. The Sangha holds particular importance for the practitioners as we could all learn a lot from the spiritual teachers.

At times you encounter seemingly nice people acting not so properly. You'd like them to change – "*the sooner the better*," you think. But look at yourself, "*How am I do-*

57

ing? What am I doing? Where am I in my life?" You will discover that you are also one of these nice people. You are trying to change, to not follow the negative tendencies, and to act positively instead. You see your own defects in the process. You will then realize that everyone has to deal with one's own negative conditions first. By engaging in the little positive acts, you begin to improve and to see more clearly. Quite naturally, your observations, reflections, and application of the Dharma will bridge your understanding of yourself to an understanding of others and vice versa.

Result is unnoticeable day to day

With Dharma practice, immediate result is usually unnoticeable. This runs contrary to our everyday experience where results are usually evident from our actions. The result of Dharma practice is different. But rest assured, some result is there and it cumulates as your practice continues. This is very important to know so you don't give up. You wish that you could see a change in yourself right away, and you don't. But after a year's practice, you look back and you will actually feel a difference in yourself. You have improved in an important way. Dharma practice is like the grass growing. You cannot see its growth from day to day. You know it is growing. Only a few days later would you see the grass visibly taller. Your state of mind is like the grass. It improves if you continue to apply the Dharma daily, practise a little a day, reflect and meditate regularly. A year later, you will feel a positive change in you.

Three important points

To the question, *"What is it that is important to me now*

that I must learn and achieve?" Here is one answer from the Tibetan:

> *"It is most important not to harm living beings.*
> *Try to help and be useful to others.*
> *And, learn to tame your mind."*

I cannot express the words as well as in Tibetan but I will try to explain the meaning. It means that we should not harm others else we will suffer negative consequences. Instead, we should try to accumulate and develop positive conditions by being helpful to others. We must also tame our mind. For now, we don't know how to apply ourselves in a positive way. We are too used to engaging in negativity due to our not knowing what to do. If we know, we would choose to act positively.

To discipline our mind is a gradual change. First, we must know our own distractions, and disturbances. They consist largely of our emotions - the emotive causes to be more precise. Without judging yourself, find out first how you feel and think. Even when you feel you are not so good, do not immediately dismiss it. You have to see it clearly to work with it. If you don't see the negatives, you can't do anything so the bad consequences will surely come your way.

The main problem is our ego clinging, a formidable root of all our emotive causes. We cannot deem it bad because it is how we are at the moment. This grasping to a self is neither good nor bad. It is just our way of experiencing ourselves as separate living beings along with all the conditions that go with the territory. This ego clinging comes about due to a mind that is confused, a mind in ignorance. It is this fundamental attachment that gives rise to samsara. As in the case where we have just stepped out of some mud, our muddied feet soil everywhere we step. Similarly, we don't wish to suffer yet we perpetuate the causes of suffering all by ourselves. The Dharma shows us the way to change totally. But until we are enlightened, our ego clinging is with us all the way.

Ego clinging gives rise to the emotive causes, such as desire/attachment, pride, jealousy, and hatred. In a way, they almost feel like a part of our basic potential. Unaware, we don't really know their effect on us. Everybody thinks feeling prideful or jealous is normal. Of course, these feelings are a part of human nature. The problem is it is also normal that they cause us to act negatively creating more suffering for everyone. We cannot escape the consequences of our own actions. Everything is subject to the law of karma. Change also comes about through action and result. Change cannot be forced. We continue to work on ourselves little by little. There is no other way.

Try not to manipulate

The emotive causes are your mind so they could be understood by you. This understanding makes you feel more at ease and peaceful. If you are calm, you can see all the constant judging and emotional states you go through. To start, the obvious emotive causes such as hatred and desire are easier to spot. If you pay closer attention, you will see other kinds of emotive causes derived from them. Try to see how each emotive cause affects you. You might notice, for instance, that you have a desire to be right. As a result, you tend to be always manipulating. You manipulate your own perspective, or the relevant facts and circumstances to suit your own feelings, in order to feel that you are right. For the most part, you are not aware that you are even doing it. For example, as soon as you sense that you might be wrong, at that same time, you manipulate whatever it is to make yourself appear right, and the others wrong. The inner adjustment is very subtle. You have to try to see how you do this. The subtle manipulation is unsettling to you and it makes you unhappy. Things appear more complicated than they actually are. It also makes you see others in a relatively negative light.

In fact, to tame the mind means not to let loose and not to be manipulative. It means not to distort your own perception. You can observe yourself when you are having a casual discussion with someone. Even when you are not sure, you try to pull in many arguments so that you could look right. Of course, when we are working with others, or trying to solve problems, it is necessary to speak up, to be clear in our communication. But here, I am alluding to those casual and benign everyday conversations. If you pay more attention, you will notice your own reactions when you are faced with the slightest contradiction. When you do see your inner jugglings, then you will know what to do. You cannot stop them in their tracks immediately. The more familiar you are with your own patterns, the less you will engage them. You will know that to distort is harmful. Naturally, when at first you can't seem to stop yourself, you will feel disappointed. Even so, keep trying to see more clearly. It will come step by step.

Once again, we need to have love, and compassion. We need to have the right understanding about karma and suffering, which is fundamental. Otherwise, we will not accept the need to change our current ways. Take, for example, the caution not to harm insects such as mosquitoes, ants, flies, and spiders. When they are regarded as pests, killing them seems justified. But if we realize that they are living beings, too, like us, our aversion towards them lessens. It does not mean that we have to like them either. We understand that they are subject to their life-conditions as insects just like we live within the human conditions. To want to stay alive is universal in all living beings. When this kind of understanding appears in you, very naturally, your wish to harm disappears. A change has occurred in you. The same applies to your inner manipulations. The shift in your perspective takes place very gradually. You could not all of a sudden adopt a different outlook even if you wanted it. There are no miracles.

6 - Mental Calm

Mental calm is one of the conditions to recognize the emotive causes and our feelings. We may understand this statement as a concept, "Yes, of course, I need this mental calm." But really we don't know why. We have not yet understood but we think we have. We file away 'the words' in a drawer for safekeeping. In this way, we delay our own understanding. As a result we have neither mental calm nor the know-how to apply it. Unless we really appreciate a need for mental calm, we would fail in our attempt to gather all the conditions to develop it. Therefore by referring to the teachings, take the time to reflect carefully whether mental calm would affect you in your own situation.

For mental calm to arise, we must first reduce our mental agitation. Agitation limits us to seeing only the surface, the grosser emotive states such as anger. But a subtler emotive cause such as jealousy or pride may very well escape our detection. When our mind is relatively calmer, we will notice the deeper emotive causes. We have to be very careful with our habit of 'always wanting'. It causes agitation. Normally when we decide to get something, we put all our energy into it; we strive for it until we get it. But this kind of approach does not work on our mind. We should neither force nor develop any tension in the mind. Any force or effort on our part will inevitably bring more tension, exactly what we don't want. Mental calm will come by itself once we truly appreciate its significance.

To let be

More than 2,500 years ago, the Buddha taught how to reach mental calm. He acknowledged that the wish to be happy is universal. Yet at the same time, unknowingly, living beings continue to create every contrary condition to happiness through their 'always wanting'. Like waves in the water, we cannot calm the water by doing anything to it. The one thing to do is to do nothing. We simply leave it. The water calms by itself. In this sense, mental calm can happen quite easily.

On the other hand, it does not mean that we can forget about mental calm by putting it away in the cupboard for instance. One misconception is to think of sleep as a state of calm. To be calm requires a presence of mind, a clear awareness that has to be developed without any action whatsoever. Mental calm is linked to a certain degree of mental clarity. What we are trying to overcome is in fact the ignorance in mind. It is like a fog that clouds our mind. What is this fog? It is the constant and endless chains of happenings in our mind. This fog will not lift simply by sitting alone somewhere. We have to be aware, which is crucial for the fog to lift.

We must be careful of our tendency to think that we have to fight the emotive causes. We are not declaring war on them, which would only bring more tension. It is a matter of proper balance. We know we need mental calm. We are really motivated yet at the same time we do not develop 'hope' for it. We have to be mindful of our hopes lest they rob us of our peace. Our desires if left unchecked could turn into greed, an excessive form of wanting. Wishing too much to be calm, we could instead develop greed, which is actually a shrinking, or a narrowing of our mind. Greed means more tension. True, we ought to be mindful of our aspiration, but at the same time, we guard against the desire. We learn to balance our positive motivation without agitation. In other words, simply be aware that mental calm is very useful, and very important. If your glasses were dirty, you'd wipe them so you could see clearly. You won't break the lens just to get rid of the dirt. It is the same with our mind. The emotive causes are in our way. They are the agitations of mind that block our perception. We don't need to fight them. We have to be aware of them and we have to understand how they function.

The Buddha said that we have a precious human existence, but it is fragile. We should use it now in a good way. By being aware and careful, we gradually move towards more clarity and calm, avoiding undue force. Tension is not an ingredient for success in anything. We should therefore be vigilant about our hopes, and urges. We train in this vigilance until it becomes a natural watchfulness for inner tensions. As we gently note their arising, in that moment we can relax. So again it is about striking a good balance between a positive aspiration and a state of mind compatible with the wanted result, mental calm.

Our well being and mental calm go hand in hand

We cannot be happy without mental calm, and we cannot develop mental calm if we are unhappy. There is a Tibetan term, which is translated as 'welfare, or well-being'. In Tibetan, by joining two words, a third is formed. The Tibetan word for 'well being' comes from the words, 'peace' and 'happiness'. Nothing is possible in the absence of either one. This means that happiness depends on ourselves only. Often, we are sad. We feel and think that something external to us will make us happy. *"If only I were richer, everything would be better. If only my spouse were nicer, I would be happier."* These thoughts and expectations reflect our errant focus and dependency on external things. On the other hand, we are not dismissing all the going-on's in the external world either. Rather, the way in which we consider and perceive the external phenomena rests solely with us. Understand that we are the source of all we perceive and we will fully appreciate with conviction how important mental calm is and its interrelatedness with our happiness, and ultimately our well-being.

Need or desire

To change, we begin with our habits now. First we separate our needs from our desires. Most of what we desire we can live without. Here, we have to be honest about what is really essential in our lives and what is nice to have. The distinction is entirely up to each individual. Nobody can tell us whether we really need something or not. This includes all the external things as well as all our inner feelings. For the moment, we are like people lost in the Sahara desert looking for an oasis. A mirage, we see it, we run after it, and when we reach it, it is gone.

Desire, one of the three main emotive causes, is like a mirage. We have to discern its true value to us rather than blindly going after it. Once we begin to question the things we hanker after, we will gradually understand their real value to us. More importantly, we will also come to understand the meaning of our desire. Then we will choose accordingly. In fact, running after a mirage in the Sahara is very frustrating. The same applies to our grasping for things yet we are totally consumed by the whole experience. If we stop running, then we will begin to calm down. We will have 'a little space' to develop our well-being, the peace and happiness we all want. The effect of the emotive causes have on us diminishes. In a way, it is not difficult to stop the 'chasing after things'. It is quite easy if we are aware.

The way to work with our desire is not to deny it as in *"I don't need this. I should avoid this."* In any case, enforcing rigid discipline does not work. But there is a simple and effective way to very gradually change the habit of desire, which takes time. Every day when we first awake, our first thought is usually connected to 'desire'. Depending on our circumstances at the time, if they are unsettling, then the first thought might be fear/worry. You should see for yourself whether this applies to you, too. It is a very subtle and subconscious feeling. But first thing in the morning, try to apply the meaning of Bodhicitta. Just think quite sincerely that you should help living beings, humans and/or animals alike. You don't need to sit in meditation. You don't have to think in details, or in any precise way. Just focus sincerely on the feeling that you want to help. *"I wish to use my capabilities as a human being to help others."* Then during the day, while attending to your work and duties, you try to always be considerate of others and help them whenever you can. In time, when this attitude becomes your habit of mind, then you have changed your desire. You will find it much easier to manage your emotions.

Being open in the present moment

In fact, alertness is actually a valued quality of well-being. It opens the present moment to us. Most of the time, we have no reason not to be happy. Rather than thinking that we are not so bad, at any given moment, we are too pre-occupied with protecting ourselves either in the future, or in the past. In fact, it is extremely rare that we have a moment where we are not caught up in the future or in the past. This means it is rare that we are in the present. The inevitable effect is we are generating hopes and fears. They then distract us to no ends. For instance, instead of being here, you may be thinking, "*Well, in a few hours time, I will be eating pizza. I'm here now but I'm hungry,*" or "*When he said that to me this morning, I should have responded this way if only I was quicker, or smarter.*" So we are never really here. And this is how we support all our tensions and emotions, which is the exact opposite of well-being. We complain often about the distractions and stress that we have. Who is in fact creating these tensions? We are. This is why to develop our well-being means to train to be in the present. If I am aware of what is happening, instead of developing tension, I am aware of its appearing. I don't have to relate it to the past. Neither do I have to protect myself in the future.

Even though we may know that we have to train to be in the here and now, often we cannot do it. Meditation is hard. The problem is we think it boring just sitting and doing nothing. But in fact, it is quite the contrary.

We just have to continue to be aware. Without pressure, we are aware. Eventually, we will begin to actually see more clearly. We will be able to see the emotive causes arising. We will start to notice our incessant thinking block us from being open to the present time. If we can be really present, the moment has a real taste, too. This discovery takes time and training. We will realize that the calmness of mind is natural. Mind is not agitated by itself. If we don't touch it, if we just let it be, then this calm will spread into our daily life as well. This could only come about if we practise, and train. This training could extend into our everyday living. In time, we will be able to discern a difference in the way we relate to people and to situations due to our calm state of mind. We will be able to see more clearly the agitations of others around us simply because we used to be like them, too. We could therefore relate to others and offer them support in a meaningful way.

7 - A Different Perpsective

The emotive causes tend to color the world around us. They make us perceive the world through their screen of multi-colors. They also condition the way we experience and react to the different situations. It is easier to see the mistakes of others because we are not in their emotions, "*It is obvious that this person should not do this, he should not do that.*" But the person himself could not really see past his emotions. We are all likewise affected. We should really try to understand that we live life through this screen. Much like wearing a pair of dark sunglasses, we always remember that our surroundings are not really as dim. We never forget that we could take off the glasses at any time. Similarly, though we are influenced by the emotive causes at the moment, we try to be aware that there is distortion. In that awareness, a small opening is there. In the least, we could choose not to follow along in our usual ways. We could weaken the filter by being aware and try to understand deeper by referring to the Dharma. Very slowly we could begin to take on a new perspective. Above all, we remain cognizant of the fact that there is in fact another way. We can take off our sunglasses and look at the sky differently.

Open to another perspective

In fact, it is not so difficult to see beyond the screen of the emotive causes. Try to see what really takes place – in us as well as in others. In fact we seldom do this. We are constantly looking out for ourselves, measuring things relative to our own advantage rather than comprehending how things truly are. But if we could walk in the others' shoes, understanding their perspectives, understanding that they also experience the same emotive causes as we do, we'd begin to be more open. We'd begin to act in concert for each other's welfare. When that happens, our whole life experience takes on an entirely new meaning. We no longer have to expend our energies entertaining frustrations. In time, our frustrations will diminish to the point that they no longer mean anything to us. There will no longer be any reasons to feel frustrated. Actually, life becomes much simpler to deal with. With less tension, and stress, our mind opens more. We can understand more and therefore we are more relaxed. Usually, we think external circumstances are our problems. But if we really look, we will find that we pile our own ideas on top of what is really happening. In fact, taking the place of others make us aware of our own grasping. Therefore, it is really worth our while to train like this, step by step.

While we try to see another's perspective, it does not mean that we should hold no personal opinions either.

The perspective of which we speak goes deeper than just surface opinions. It is natural for people to have different points of view. The problem is our quickness to judge and to reject. We tend to think that when one is right, then the other must be wrong. And our feeling of 'wrong' often translates into a feeling of opposition in us, and then we reject the other. In fact, reality is not like that at all. You are right. The other can also be right. Both sides could be right at the same time. Different realities can coexist saddled with the different views and conditions of people. But, our clinging wants others to follow us. They should change to agree with us. Often we tense up, our mind narrows, which is totally unnecessary. By opening ourselves to others, we will come to realize that many solutions or interpretations are equally valid. Different realities can coexist in an openness of minds.

Therefore, we should try to move away from a 'black/white' interpretation of situations and of people. We don't like conflicts. On the other hand, we don't have to accept nor reject the conflict, or differing points of view. We don't have to change our viewpoint either. There is no sacrifice or surrendering of our own views. We simply recognize that it is perfectly normal that people do hold different views. We will then be willing to take the time to understand. We try to see the circumstances, the conditions the other party is in. This will shed light on the situation from a different angle. In fact, this exchange is often satisfying because it opens us to a solution suitable for everyone. Our habit is to think of things and situations quite solidly. It is either this way or no other way. One side is right and the other side is wrong. If we invest sincere interest and concern in the other's position, we will see more carefully and more deeply. In this way, a conflict can become a source of happiness for us. How? The conflict affords us the chance to be considerate of others, a chance to seek a solution to satisfy them, which is at the heart of our Bodhicitta practice. Very spontaneously, we are stepping away from our ego-centredness.

A fertile field for wisdom to grow

A common error of judgment we make is to think that we are already too old to change. We have missed the boat. We feel that we have already wasted a lot of time. This is not true because our past is full of valuable experiences. They show us the errors we have made due to the influence of the emotive causes. If we could understand how the emotions confused us in the past and marred our judgments and actions, it is already a very big step. The past is our fertile field if we know how to farm it. It belongs to us. You may ask, "*What will it yield then?*" It is 'yeshe' in Tibetan, or 'wisdom'. Here, wisdom does not equate to intelligence, but clarity of mind. In fact, this wisdom can remove the dust on our glasses so we could see much clearer. Little by little, we reflect on our past mistakes. We start to recognize how our emotions affected us in our thinking and actions. Seeing clearer, slowly and gradually, we could start to adjust our ways to avoid the same mistakes. It is clear seeing that allows us to make the adjustments; we are in effect, weakening the emotive causes. This enables our mind to become clearer and our wisdom to develop.

Non-distraction is necessary

To help us reflect properly and to grow this clarity of mind that is wisdom, what has to be developed is a state of non-distraction. 'Non-distraction' is a better translation than the word, 'concentration'. It shows directly the need to 'just let be' without any involvement with the distractions. It connotes a sense of not going anywhere but be here in the moment, to be in the presence of what is really taking place now. This non-distraction can be carried through straight into our daily activities. You could be a mediator between two people arguing. Look at the emotions involved. Do not follow them. Do not get drawn into them. Simply look and try to understand what is really taking place. This shows how the emotions affect us. Then try to diffuse the argument to help the two parties to reconcile. You will appreciate how useful it is to see without the distraction of the emotions. This is one way to develop wisdom. We have an endless source of opportunity to grow our wisdom because the emotions are abundant in all of us. We will never run out of opportunities.

Qualities of an observer attitude

What has been described is basically an attitude of 'an observer'. Note, however, that this attitude does not include any judgment or criticism. It is neither apathy nor non-involvement where problems are viewed as exclusively as 'theirs'. It is a view where everything is possible, and anything can happen. There is nothing which is really good, and nothing which is really bad either. Everything can happen. In this scenario, we need only to see clearly what is happening. If we could do something to help, of course we act without hesitation. Yet we are detached because everything just happens. We do not judge others, their behavior, or their situations. This does not mean we care only to develop ourselves either. The point is to expand our awareness. In this context, we can become more balanced. We are alert, not asleep or drowsy. We are relaxed. Relaxed does not mean to for example, to physically lie on a sofa and eat sweets and cakes all afternoon. We can be relaxed and energetic at the same time. Our goal is to attain this state of mind ever fresh, available, clear, and relaxed. A mind relaxed is happy. It is not the ordinary happiness, which is fleeting, but a deeper happiness inseparable from the deep serenity or clarity of mind. It is there even in times of sadness because it is our innate nature. Though it is not yet the state of a perfected Buddha, it is pretty close to it.

8 - Contentment

If we are astute in our daily awareness training, we will notice an element missing in our overall state of well-being, something very important - it is 'contentment'. The emotions often frustrate and disturb us so it is important that we find some balance. Contentment is that vital link to stability. However, we are not at all used to it. A tiny little thing could make us angry. In fact, it is when contentment is forgotten that we fall victim to our emotions. We develop all kinds of wanting, which run contrary to feeling satisfied.

For example, a teacher is sitting comfortably sheltered under the tent. Inside, it is dry, there is no wind. The air is fresh, and the temperature just perfect. The only problem is the sound system. There is no microphone or loudspeakers so he has to speak loudly for everyone to hear him. He could feel content enough considering the good conditions. Or he could lose his composure and feel irritated over the lack of proper sound equipment. It is up to him. The externals are as they are. But how he feels is dependent on him.

In the presence of every emotive cause, such as jealousy, contentment is absent. Its absence affects us in different ways and actually gives rise to the emotive causes. What we are referring to is more than a wanting of basic material things. Most of us are fortunate enough to have all the basic necessities of life. Our feelings of inadequacies come from us. Why then are we not content? Basically, we are not even aware that discontentment breeds the emotions. There is really no need to feel dissatisfied but all the messages we get from our families, friends and the society at large is everything but that. On the contrary, since when we were children, we were always told to work for all kinds of things. We should get this, get that, and so on. Inadvertently, the bar of our expectations and desires has been raised so high that contentment is out of sight. In fact we are so preoccupied with our constant wanting that we don't see that we're not satisfied. Generally, the dissatisfaction is unconscious. The whole point of trying to be content is to reduce the grasping enough so that we could begin to decipher for ourselves this feeling of 'lack' - where does it come from and how it affects us. This is why first, we want to be aware of our lack of contentment, and then we could begin to develop it.

Connect to Bodhicitta

To avoid falling into this trap of discontent, we try always to be connected to Bodhicitta. We wish everyone happiness and not to have to suffer. This is not just an idea, but a genuine and complete openness to the welfare of others. It is also not just an occasional attitude we remember from time to time. Rather, it is very crucial to align ourselves with this enlightened attitude in every moment. Otherwise, dissatisfaction could easily creep in and we are caught up in ourselves again. Especially we have to be vigilant and apply Bodhicitta in our relationships with our family. You love your family - you love your spouse, your children, your parents, and so on, however, the most intense tensions and feelings are also right there in these relationships. Generally, you are able to cope at work. You know you don't have to love your colleagues. It is very nice if you like them but then, you think the point is to be able to work together to get the job done. But to you, family is different. You are supposed to love them. Due to this notion of obligation, you don't really see clearly what is taking place. You feel more the reason to be emotional, because you think you are acting out of love. For example, when you are arguing with your child, remember the Bodhicitta you are supposed to be connected to...it is simply forgotten. "*It might be good this way*" often turns into "*it must be this way*". You are especially demanding where your child's health or safety is concerned. But you are not really aware of your own demand. To you, it is not a demand but the only way. There is this complete change in you where your child's 'own good or benefit' has become in fact 'your own good' where you are the 'judge'. And you want everything to be perfect, i.e. your way exactly. You have lost your awareness, you have forgotten the open mind of Bodhicitta, and all kinds of problems can begin right there.

To be more understanding of others

If we do not wish to be so disturbed by the emotive causes, then we have to start to perceive others in a different light. We have to see them essentially like us. They don't want to suffer, and they want to be happy. We are not perfect and neither are they. We have a strong tendency to think that somehow we are better than others. *"I'm working so hard and he is so lazy!"* In fact, we all have the same faults, and qualities. Again, contentment has a role to play here. We have to learn to be satisfied with other people just the way they are. This we can usually agree with, to a certain extent when we apply it to the population at large. We understand that people are people. Where it starts being difficult is with our close relatives and family. For example, a father finds it hard to accept that his son is not perfect, or that a son could not possibly be a copy of his father. In theory, we can all agree that nobody is perfect. Therefore, a son who is not perfect should not come as a surprise! But in general, you want your children to think and behave like you. Contentment is forgotten, and you are not open to accept your children for who they are. You may find fault even with some of their positive qualities. You should give them a chance to develop in the way they want. Allow your children to grow and develop their own way. In the meantime, we expend our efforts into developing our own openness and contentment.

The training is to look at the instances in our mind during the day. Many of our pre-occupations are not necessary. We will see this. We can then relax. This understanding and perception will come to us naturally. There is no need to try to force it. There is no point to analyze everything either. Simply be present and look at the events without our opinions, and prejudices piled on top of them. Just look without judging. Then our perception will be clearer and more precise. Without this unbiased perception, we will not be able to see the emotions coming. So the real training is to just take the time to look at the ideas and thoughts in our mind—not judge them, and the understanding will come.

9 - Some Benefits of Meditation

Alongside with Bodhicitta, meditation is essential to effectively deal with the emotive causes. Our state of mind is very subtle and sensitive. Try as we may, it is very difficult for us to change. Meditation clarifies our mind so we could understand in a deeper and more precise way. The process is gradual whereby our understanding expands until it reaches the all-knowing state of a Buddha.

When we begin the practice of meditation, we simply sit and meditate. Some people think that results of meditation are all the same. From my own experience and reflections, I did not come to the same conclusion. Without a basic knowledge of the Dharma, meditation affects us somewhat differently. I have found that our attention must be properly directed during meditation to develop greater clarity with proper understanding.

Some people think, "*I know already...that my emotions*

can disturb me and cause me to act negatively...but I can't help it. I cannot change." You know you feel like this from time to time. When you are angry, you feel you cannot avoid it. However, if you follow the Dharma's advice and meditate, you will begin to see differently. Due to the practice, when your anger appears even if you cannot change it, you might feel, *"The Dharma tells me that I cannot see clearly due to the ignorance in my mind. I was unaware of the emotive causes when they came up. They got out of control and now I am so angry. I'm suffering this anger and I'm also making the people around me suffer. What's more, I'm creating negative karma, for myself and others."* This shows that you are already a bit clearer. You might be able to describe this process to your friends right now. You could repeat the words and think you really know the meaning. You understand and agree with it all. But when it comes down to the actual application, you find it difficult to handle your mind's situation. You are at a loss. This is why meditation is essential. It takes time, a very long time. But if you continue day by day, your mind's understanding will no doubt improve. Gradually, you will get the meaning of all the teachings and methods. More importantly, you will be able to practise and apply them.

Meditation is being in the present moment. Since all moments are the same in a constant continuum, given any situation, time or place, be it sitting on a cushion in a meditation hall, or in the arena of daily living, we can remain ever present. Without force, we try to be aware during the day the same as in our meditation. We apply it whenever we can. Gradually our awareness improves. There are no fragments of time that we practise or we don't practise. Our practising awareness brings clarity directly into our daily life. In fact, there is no real benefit unless it takes place in our everyday experience. This is very important to understand. Of course, we cannot do it right away. Again, without undue pressure, we try little by little to become increasingly aware of our hopes and expectations. Our frustrations and tensions will diminish. We could then appreciate why it is so important to bring everything into the awareness in every moment. Every day of our life is our field of awareness. Awareness does not have to stop. And it is meditation that trains this awareness.

Gampopa's advice is to first take refuge, and then the Bodhisattva Vow. Meditation comes after. This process gives the proper direction. We have to learn the meaning of Refuge and the Bodhisattva aspiration and action. In this way, we will come to really feel the meaning of the Dharma. When we then engage in meditation, we will understand how to follow the instructions. If someone were to just sit and meditate without any view or orientation, there is not much sense in it. Actually, meditation depends on some qualities of character, too. This is why Bodhicitta, conscientious effort, knowing how to relax, and the right expectations are all needed.

Here is one understanding that you will gain through meditation. The teachings explain that every problem comes from mind. You might not agree with it totally thinking "...*but it can't be just me, it's also the other people who are causing the problem. Without them, I'd be OK*." But actually, even if you stay quietly by yourself, you'd still have a problem. You'd want to be with other people. We have all felt this strange contradiction. It is meditation that will allow you to see for yourself that each problem does arise within you. The understanding comes through meditation. Otherwise, you will find this very difficult to believe.

Another understanding you can gain from meditation is about fear. Due to our very strong habit of self-grasping, we are absorbed in ourselves. We always feel, *"I want to get something out of this. I am afraid of losing. I don't want to lose. I must not lose."* The worrying escalates in your mind unconsciously into dread, then outright fear. Through the meditation, you will realize that it is your own grasping that produces the fear. This will make it easier for you to cope. We all want to be free but we also want to hang on to our desires. But if we could really see our desire, then we'd realize that there is nothing to lose. Our state of mind becomes freer, stronger and more powerful when compared to the mind trapped in desire/fear. Words, concepts, and intellectualizations won't show you how to actually work with your mind or your emotions. You have to see for yourself how you function and this is why meditation is so important.

10 - A daily practice

Once we understand the importance of Bodhicitta and meditation, we reflect deeper to increase this understanding and to apply it in our daily life. We understand that genuine love and compassion towards all sentient beings arises out of a true discernment of the universal conditions we are in. Knowing that ignorance dominates our minds and affects all our thoughts and actions, pleasant or unpleasant, we realize that things are not so simple due to our own 'not knowing. For now, we are projecting all kinds of illusions, and ever so naturally, we react and generate both positive and negative actions. It is therefore perfectly normal that at any given time, a person could hold good or bad thoughts. This understanding releases us from our judgmental attitudes towards people. We also don't have to take things so personally ourselves. We could then really feel love and compassion for any individual. All the emotive causes like our pride and jealousy appear manageable. When that happens we experience the immediate benefit of the ability to see clearly what is really happening, i.e. the karmic causes and conditions influencing every living being.

To be able to see clearly, it is very important that we listen and reflect carefully the exact meaning of the teachings. We are used to loading our mind with information yet neglecting to get the proper meaning. We may get by like this with general and everyday things, but when it comes to the Dharma, a very precise and proper understanding is a must. Our obscurations are strong due to the emotive causes, tendencies, habits, and wrong concepts. In order to see exactly all the conditions, we have to look again and again, very carefully. The best way to train is to apply the teachings in our daily life to really see what is the truth, and what is important. In this way, step by step, our understanding will deepen.

When you don't know clearly your situation, you simply continue what you have been doing all along, and everything seems copasetic on the surface. Life goes on regardless of whether you choose to be aware or not. If you are aware, then a solution to your problematic circumstances becomes conceivable. Lodged in the emotive causes, karmic conditions, and suffering, to see clearly all the details of our conditions is undeniably a real challenge to us. We want to try to see what are the causes to events in our lives. We try to connect the results to their causes. While it is very difficult to apprehend all the intricacies of cause and effect, they are nonetheless the natural conditions of life. Through a precise understanding of the meaning of the Dharma in our personal experience, we will appreciate how important regular practice is as the vital underpinning to our ability to cope with clarity all the conditions of life. Change cannot be forced. We have to see reality, and only through its recognition can real change take place.

Be present at the start and end of each day

In the morning, when we first awake, our mind is heavy and unclear. This is a habit of mind. The meaning of practice is to be present and clear. It is very important to know that we should be present and clear for as much as possible. When we are unclear, it is like moving in heavy traffic in the morning to get to work. We are moving. We are seeing many things yet we are not discovering anything. This is what a foggy mind is like.

First thing in the morning, or whenever possible, take a few seconds, and tell yourself, "*Hey, wake up.*" Of course, you don't have to say the words. The point is to really try to have presence of mind, and to feel that you are here. And if you are already practising regularly, then just try to connect with the meaning of practice. In the beginning, it is hard to remember to be present. Just try to connect with its meaning as much as you can. This in-itself already indicates that you are somewhat clearer. In the beginning, you will forget. Why? You are not used to it. Instead, you are used to being heavy, you can't help but follow your tendencies. But try to apply a little effort and gently remind yourself from time to time. This will train your mind in the 'how to be present'. And you will learn to apply presence of mind increasingly. This is usually what we call 'meditation'. If we meditate regularly, we will find it quite easy to have presence of mind. If not, when you wake up in the morning, remind yourself. Be present. Then try to reflect that you'd like to use your capacity to be helpful to everyone, to support the people that you are with. It should not be a forced commitment either, because more problems would then be created. Go very naturally, in one way it is simple, "*I will do what I can.*" Just before you go to sleep at night, repeat the same kind of awareness and reflection again. This does not mean however, that you try to meditate while lying down. Rather, the point is to be present again to dedicate your day's efforts towards benefiting others. This is how you connect to the meaning of the Dharma at the beginning and at the end of each day.

Good for myself and good for others

Being 'human' is very precious. Individually we should think, "*I should do something useful and good for myself and for others as well.*" Although this is a basic attitude the Dharma encourages it is at the same time, a concept that comes quite naturally to us all. Nobody ever thinks, "*I should be bad and I want to worsen!*" Everybody thinks, "*I want to improve and be good all the time.*" But then, what is 'good' depends on how you feel. The Dharma explains that 'good for myself' means, "*I am able to properly use my capacity and my current good conditions in this life and in all future lives*". This means that we should not be self-grasping. We try to be open to others. As explained already, we understand that others are like us and so we help them too. If we could maintain and apply this view regularly, we will soon come to realize the meaning of the Dharma. Dealing with our emotive causes then becomes straightforward because we can see what is important, and necessary for everyone.

Understanding gives space

When we want to learn, we listen carefully. We think we need to connect with our wisdom. We think we want to get rid of the emotions. We feel that they cause us a lot of problems. But these ideas are again a form of strong grasping. Again, our emotive causes are stirred up. We feel unsettled. But real understanding of the natural process of cause and effect softens our attitudes and feelings. Although very subtly the strong grasping is still there, there is at the same time, also a little more openness of mind that we could apply. At the moment, we don't see very much. Our mind is very tight linked to all the conditions that arise due to our wanting. We always feel that there are so many things to do. We thus feel very heavy and tight. All the concepts, emotions, and distractions accompanying us are very strong. Of course, we could still be aware of the emotive causes despite the tightness, but we could not change our reactions to them. They come back again and again. We need the little space to see and to understand properly and then change could happen quite spontaneously.

Shamar Rinpoche always says, "*Be flexible, your mind.*" Flexible means to be a little open, then things are easier to deal with. But to be flexible is very difficult. Again, you need the proper understanding of the fundamental conditions of beings. Some of us know already but we don't really apply our knowledge. Why not? Because we don't know exactly. The concepts in our mind therefore seem very complicated. They become simpler, and easier when we see them very clearly. It is in meditation that our mind can become very clear. A clear mind is problem free. Therefore, in a clear mind, all the emotive causes are no longer problematic.

For example, you are in a room with the window opened. A big bee flies in. Observe in yourself whether you are tight, or open and flexible. If you are used to being considerate of other living beings, naturally you will not be too scared. You may still dislike the bee and decide to chase it out. On the other hand, if you don't consider the bee a sentient being, then you may panic. The reactions vary among people. Some people get angry. Some hurt the bee while others choose to kill it. Ask yourself, *"Why do I feel so panic stricken?"* or *'Why do I feel so hostile towards the bee?"* The answer is there if you have the Dharma as your reference. For someone connected with the Dharma, he could see, *"Ah yes, it's because I am too focused and concerned about myself. This is why I feel so frightened or angry."* When you look to understand, many things will appear. You should think more carefully and you will come to understand differently the meaning of being 'tight' versus 'being flexible'. You are not asked to like insects such as bees, flies, ticks, or mosquitoes either, it comes back to a basic understanding of why you react the way you do.

Introspect daily

Whether our mind is open or tight is more a habit of mind. We are not born with it yet we don't see that we are constantly engaged in all kinds of projections. By being aware changes our vision slightly. We have a chance to think a little deeper. We could reflect by questioning ourselves:

"What is love?"

"What is compassion?"

"What is suffering?"

"What is a negative thought and the kinds of action it causes?"

"What is a positive thought and the kinds of action it triggers?"

In the beginning, the answers are not clear. Nevertheless, from time to time, reflect and introspect by yourself. In lieu of thinking in generality as in 'all sentient beings', try to analyze your interactions with actual people in your life. During the normal course of a day, through your interactions with people, your family, relatives, friends, or colleagues, you could observe the many emotive causes arising in you. Observe how they make you feel. Ask yourself why you have to feel the way you do. Observe in yourself how the emotive causes affect your behavior and attitudes towards others, and your actions and choices. In this way, you could become much clearer as to how you function. Slowly, it is this kind of awareness that gives you some freedom of mind. Gradually, the answers will become clearer and more meaningful. You will learn slowly to work with them. Your state of mind will gradually be more open, and easier to change for the better. There is no need to scrutinize constantly your feelings, your relationships with others, or your actions. Just occasionally, try to be aware without pressure. From time to time, reflect on what it means to be good to one another. In time, through a lessening of your projections, you will see more clearly the emotive causes. Then you will know how to manage them and how to adjust yourself.

The introspection process if engaged daily and regularly will strengthen your mind's capacity. Your confidence will grow. How? The teachings tell us that if we can see the negatives in what we do, in how we apply ourselves through our feelings, then we will see why we make mistakes. When we do, we may feel guilty and upset. We may lose trust and faith in ourselves. But, due to our awareness, we then apply understanding. We will start to feel that we could behave differently and we could try to handle all our tendencies of mind. Then already, we will feel more reassured. Very gradually, our confidence will grow affording us some liberation of mind - in this context, our mind feels lighter, and much easier to manage.

For example, in your family life when things are generally working out smoothly, some tensions are inevitably there. Some slight anger is always connected with tension. It is not heavy. You usually try to just ignore it or avoid it. You keep it inside and you leave it alone. But what you are asked to do here is to reflect on why you get angry? Why do you feel irritated? What is the reason? *"It's because other people are not acting properly,"* is a common response. People are not acting according to your wishes so you get angry. It's about the little things, the little conditions. *"OK! I'll just leave it and I won't say anything."* You feel like this constantly and you are a little unhappy due to your anger. Try to find out why. When you don't have the Dharma to guide you, you are at a loss to explain why you are like this. Due to the ignorance, you cannot see too clearly. But following the teachings, you begin to look closer at the roots of your feelings. You begin to pay attention to the emotive causes. The most common ones are desire, pride, unmet expectations, and jealousy. Go a bit deeper, and you will see the grasping and the excessive focus on your 'self' underlying the emotive causes. Then slowly, you will start to understand how they could disturb, or confuse you, how they could cloud your perception.

Too much self-focus is not good

As you continue to introspect, you will discover that too much self-focus disturbs you. It makes you suffer. *"If I could only let go of this self-clinging then I won't have to suffer anymore."* But you cannot let go and so all the little irritations and unpleasantness continue to appear. The suffering is like the dust that collects in our house. It's always there. The dust is not harmful but it accumulates. If we don't clean regularly, our house will become very dirty. The suffering of self-focus is not great but it's there. If unattended to, it could grow into great suffering. Reflect on any one day and you will find that from morning to night, there is always some suffering. There is always something wrong. Unconsciously, we project our ideas and thoughts onto things and people and we are critical of them. Even if you set aside a day to do nothing but sit, you will get bored. You'd want to do something. These kinds of unpleasantness we definitely have everyday. By introspecting regularly, you will soon realize that the tensions are all related to you. They concern small trivia that are of no real importance to you. When you could see for yourself, you'd want to let them go. However, it still won't just happen on the spot.

As to other people

You may think, *"Yes, I can see my part but what about the other people? I can be quiet but what if people won't leave me alone?"* We know we've all thought like this. *"I try to be nice but the other person just won't let me be!"* But if you really see that the basic problem is the connection to the emotive causes and the very subtle and subconscious feelings that they trigger in you, if you really see very clearly this inner functioning inside you, then you will understand why other people do not behave quite properly. Everybody is the same. Everybody has feelings, good or bad. Everybody connects to the emotive causes like pride, and jealousy due to the ignorance in the mind, and then very naturally acts under their influence. So instead of thinking, "*I don't understand how he could be like that,*" you realize that you do understand. Immediately you will feel more space in your mind, more relaxed, and less suffering. The emotions will continue to appear in you. It is wrong to expect that the emotive causes will disappear. They will continue to arise but they will be much softer, and manageable

Somehow, when you really understand the meaning of Bodhicitta, you will think, "*I should try to help others instead of just following how I feel.*" If you could apply these attitudes, then you will become more flexible in handling your emotive causes. Flexible means more understanding, lighter, and resistant to going astray. You no longer react impulsively to an emotive cause as it appears. Instead, there is a space so you could respond more appropriately. If you could really apply step by step this openness of mind, then you'd see and understand the negativities in others being due to the underlying emotive causes which could arise in you as well. This is a very important point.

Perk up our interest

It is difficult to watch ourselves all the time. But we can, on a regular basis, be more alert during the course of a day. Each time we detect a good or bad feeling, it tells us about us. It could actually be an interesting learning experience. We cannot get the meaning right away because we are not very clear. Life can be pleasurable, nice, comfortable, and joyful. Life can also be fearful, problematic, distracting, judgmental, depressing, and sad.

These are regular conditions of life. These conditions also taint our perceptions and weigh us down. We all want to learn how to live life. Start with our everyday experiences. Try to understand by connecting with the meaning of the teachings. When our mind is focused as such, the more we look, the more we will apprehend why we feel the way we do. And we can learn from both good and bad experiences alike. It is through our interest in something that it becomes useful to us. If you are interested in studying plants, everywhere you go, you will notice them. They naturally appear in your view. But we have to go through the learning process. Try to really understand how we are, why we react and respond in the way we do relative to the emotive causes. In time, we will realize that we are improving very naturally - like the grass, its growth is not noticed until after a few days.

To look at yourself does not imply that you will see extraordinary things about you. In fact it means to see all the ordinary and regular ways in which you think and function daily. It is to see your normal ideas, thoughts, and feelings. There are no special times that you set aside just to learn about yourself. Ignorance in the mind does not appear during a special part of the day, it is your mind now. As explained already, when you are just starting to train, you try to look when your emotions are not so intense. Later on, the intense emotional causes will also prove useful. The trouble is when the problems are small, you tend to ignore them out of habit. This is wrong. You should beware of the little things. Your mind when only slightly disturbed, where consequences are not of significant matter to you is an ideal ground to grow and multiply your understanding about your own functioning. Start easy, and then later on you can tackle the heavier issues.

Apply Bodhicitta

Life is not easy and we are always faced with difficulties. They are connected with our desires. We don't want to be disturbed yet the natural conditions of our mind now always disturb us. We want material things and activities to do. We have goals and we are constantly in pursuit of them. We have to relate to people all the time, our family, friends, or associates at the workplace. We could begin to apply a different orientation or attitude. Instead of focusing exclusively on our own gains, or making sure that we are not losing out, we could try to be considerate of other people's needs and aspirations while still looking after our own interests. I believe, *"It's not easy but you can do it."* Due to your kindness, and openness, your actions will be much more positive. Your communication with others will be much more effective. You will become stronger. Maybe it'd take longer to actually see some results, they will be there without question. This is just one possible way to begin the practice of Bodhicitta.

Individual learning and discovery

It is easy to talk about Bodhicitta as an idea. But since everyone is busily engaged in one's own responsibilities, it is difficult to find space for Bodhicitta. Some confusion is there when you think, *"I should only think about what I should do?"* The teachings tell us that we must find for ourselves what to do. You will have many questions. The Buddha said, *"You should not be naïve. You have to be clear!"* Of course, you are encouraged to refer to the Dharma for some answers. Then very slowly, you try to learn about your own inner attitudes. Because people are all different each with unique sets of conditions, circumstances, and situations, nobody could tell you what you should do. It always comes back to your finding out what works for you, what makes sense for you. Your own discovery is much clearer, and more effective than someone else telling you to do this, or that.

In the beginning, some confusion is to be expected. But very slowly, you will be able to discern the different meanings because certain directions are already explained in the teachings. For example, it is important to be aware of the emotive causes, as they are the roots of our emotions. Another direction is to support one another in lieu of being selfish and greedy. By habit, you tend to be greedy. By being increasingly aware, you will discover this about you. Whenever you are trying to support others, but you feel tense, uncomfortable, and closed-off, that is the time to try to figure out the reason. Is it due to your anger, or expectations? You will see a little more clearly. *"Ah, this is because I am greedy. This is because I am grasping too much to myself!"* Then you will know how to adjust by yourself. You will feel your original concerns unnecessary and unimportant giving you only suffering in turn.

There is kindness in everyone

When you look, you will find it difficult. You feel a tug of war inside you, back and forth. You are following your habits and your tendencies. Characteristic of being in samsara, you have attachments, expectations, and fears on the one hand. On the other, being human, you have kindness. When you apply awareness, you will feel this kindness naturally in you. But you are oscillating between the two sides especially in the beginning. But if you stay and continue with your awareness, you will begin to see and understand. You will find that even someone who appears to be really negative is still somehow 'kind' relative to his perspective. It is his perspective that has gone awry due largely to his inability to see clearly. When you see this, your compassion will develop equally towards all beings.

Do not discriminate

At the moment, you find some people nice and others not so nice. You feel compassion for the nice people in hardships but not for those you think are acting negatively. This is discrimination. It makes it difficult for you to balance your mind when you discriminate. Therefore, it is easier in the morning, before you are in the thick of things, to start by connecting with love and compassion. To apply Bodhicitta seems always more difficult. But if you begin to apply it little by little, and get its meaning through your own everyday experiences, then this is very beneficial. Your mind will become very clear, and very stable.

The Dharma does not insist that you 'have to' be equally compassionate towards all beings. The Dharma states that it is possible for you to see the conditions for beings, and when you do, you will feel compassion for them. Your mind is much clearer, more peaceful. Your understanding increases so you are able to act differently than what you are used to. You will act with less discrimination much like a doctor who treats all patients equally who would not turn away a patient as in, "*I will not treat him because he is a bad person.*" There is no selection involved.

Each of us has to decide to learn about the truth of the Dharma. Each of us has to want to be useful and less distracted. The question is, "*How do I do it? I am try-ing but my conditions are not so straightforward or easy. What should I do?*" Then we should call to mind the im-portance of meditation. We should meditate. If we do it regularly, then slowly, we become increasingly aware. Meditation will gradually become a habit of mind. Out-side of meditation, our honed awareness ushers in clear-er perceptions and understanding. Then step by step, we will be able to be free from the emotive causes.

Conclusion
Work with and not against the emotive Causes

Only we can decide whether we want to take the time and the effort to be aware. Nobody can be aware for us. At the same time, we have to accept others for who they are and not focus exclusively on their faults. We have faults, too. We practise contentment and try to see clearer. We have a little more space so we could have a chance to react appropriately to each situation. To react appropriately means to act in a way to improve things for all concerned. Acting in this way will not generate frustrations because we are thinking for others. Where there is no ego-clinging, there can be no frustration. Therefore, everything depends on us. It is a question of *"What can I do about me so that things do not have to be so painful or difficult?"* We will begin to appreciate that acting positively creates peace and happiness for everyone. Always remember that if we are careless, there will be problems. And if we take care, the results will be much more positive.

We try to act and react in a reasonable way, with good sense and proportion. Try not to be so absolute in our expectations of things and people, which is how we are most of the time. We are very unwilling to accept compromises. We don't accept that everything could have many 'faces'. Seldom do we acknowledge that differing views and approaches could lead to good results. Our tunnel vision narrows and limits the possibilities out there and set us up for conflict and argument. In fact, different sides could be appeased and satisfied if we act for the welfare of others. Other people's aspirations and wishes are also valuable, and important. We will also realize that there are many solutions to things; these possibilities are now open to us. We could choose to act in a way where there will be more happiness all around.

In any difficult or painful situation, the same principle applies. More often than not, we do not step back to see how to deal with the situation. We are transfixed into our thinking that it should be a certain way. We do not allow any space. We are entangled in our attachments. *"It is MY wife who is suffering from cancer. This situation affects ME in this way."* In lieu of egocentric seeing, look for a basic way to solve a problem. The case of teenage children addicted to street drugs seems to have originated primarily from a problem in communication. Instead of pushing one's own ways, step back and reestablish the communication between parents and children first. Without engendering Bodhicitta, it is very difficult. When we try to help a cancer sufferer, we cannot prevent his imminent death. We could help to diminish his despair, his anguish, and to relieve his actual suffering. To remedy a disease is important but it should not cover up the importance of helping the diseased person. Therefore, in any situation, pulling back to see more clearly will prove very useful.

Sometimes when our emotions are very strong already, we feel very frustrated because there is little we could do. We feel as if it is too late. This happens all the time. Our expectation is the problem. We have to be realistic. We know we are not yet realized and that is not a problem. For now, we just try to be aware of the emotive cause as it arises, just to see it. It will dissipate without our interference. Simply recognize it and leave it alone. Do not fight it. Have no expectations. If we expect anything at all, we will meet with frustration.

In an art gallery, we see many paintings and artwork from ancient times right up to the present day. Some are good, and others are not so good. Suppose there is a painting with only a few color patches on it valued at a few million dollars. At first glance, you cannot fathom its given value. After studying more about art and paintings, the understanding gained may make you appreciate why that painting is considered so distinguishing. After a few more years, you may actually develop a genuine experience of its beauty directly. It could have been studying, learning, understanding, recognizing, and appreciation, that you have grown to experience the beauty of the painting first hand. Our recognition of an emotive cause is the same. We need education, practice, and experience. The culmination of all three does not come after a few minutes, days, or months. It comes only after continuous, and extensive training - just as it is for any musical virtuosity, or professional training. It takes time, and it takes experience to see the emotive causes as they are. Don't forget that our habitual tendencies have been with us all our lives. For most of us, it means at least twenty years. Add to that the many previous lifetimes we have had, our habits are indeed ingrained. Change will certainly not come easily but it is definitely possible.

In dealing with emotive causes, we always go back to the very basics. We practise awareness as much as we can. We do not fight the emotions; instead, we use the mind's energy differently through Bodhicitta. When we are clear, our complicated ideas and thoughts somehow are reduced to very simple basics. We place our trust in the nature of our mind. We are aware of the emotive causes. We don't fight them, neither our own nor others'. At all times, we try to see clearer so that we give ourselves the chance to avoid mistakes. It takes time to see but then it works. This training in everyday life will make everything simpler. But we have to start the training. We have to begin to experience it step by step, and we will understand how it works. It is not a story that you tell or one that you remember. It is something that you have to experience for yourself. You may repeat the wonderful details you have heard about the North Pole but until you have actually traveled there, you don't know it as it is. In the same way, you have to train every day through your own experience of every day—step by step, little by little. Then, the meaning will become clear to you.

Question and Answer

Question: Given the fact that young people, or teenagers have strong emotions, how could we help them to work with their emotions? How much freedom could be allowed for their own experimentation with their emotions without dire consequences?

Answer: Young people do not like it when people interfere in their lives and experiences. When you give them rules, they will try to break them, or to get around them. It is therefore not recommended to restrict them with all kinds of rules. We do not dictate to them any rules or value judgments. We could talk about how to develop the awareness of the emotions, and how to deal with them. We do not state what is right or what is wrong. We could discuss the methods of awareness with them. But we let them live the experiences by themselves. They will have many experiences. If they apply some awareness, they will slowly learn to integrate it into their daily experiences of life. Only they can create their own experiences. The only thing that we could do is just to teach them how to recognize and deal with the emotions.

With respect to the handling of the emotive causes and emotional feelings, what applies to adults is essentially the same for teenagers. There are no external rules because rules and boundaries are exactly the opposite of openness. Rather, each individual has to develop within his inner consciousness a universal reference of what is acceptable, and what is not acceptable. This reference is very close to what we know as ethic. We have to really see, and listen precisely to understand clearly what is taking place, and its meaning. We step away from our life now, which seems to be on autopilot without clear awareness. We take back control and really connect to what is occurring and taking the time to see precisely. Our mind may be somewhat obscured right now, and it is not that easy to understand what is happening. But if we continue to practise awareness, then gradually, we will become clearer. It will become easier. We don't have to struggle as hard somehow. We are more at ease with ourselves. Then in time, the emotions will not disturb us anymore.

A traveler who spends time interacting with the locals will get to understand them. Someone who is just passing through the same country in a train just looking at the landscape, and not stopping anywhere, will not get to know its people. We, too, have to spend the time to stop and take note of our emotions. We do not just ride through them without ever knowing the details about them, where they come from, or where they go.

Indifference is a closed state of mind. There is no feeling involved—almost like dead. Equanimity, on the other hand, is an open and balanced state ready to tackle any situation, or any feeling that arises. It is very much alive. We respond always with Bodhicitta. Good or bad, we respond without judging. The Bodhicitta attitude makes possible this unbiased open mind.

We often think what is the use of suffering? Look at physical pain. It is very necessary and important because it signals to us that something is wrong. A toothache tells us a tooth is decaying. It is the same with suffering. When we experience it, it tells us that we have gone wrong somewhere along the way. Most of the time, we act blindly unaware of our mistakes. When we run into a snag, "*Oh, where did I go wrong?*" We have to learn how to prevent the suffering. It is as simple as brushing our teeth to stave off cavity. Toothaches are useful signs yet we are not saying that you have to go looking for a toothache. It is just that we, individually, have to learn the methods of how to prevent the suffering, and then to practise them.

Publishing finished
in October 2019 by Pulsio
Publisher Number : 4006
Legal Deposit : October 2019
Printed in Bulgaria